## Obituaries

# Julia Randall

NORTH BENNINGTON — Julia Randall, distinguished poet, teacher and environmental activist, died at her home in North Bennington on Sunday. The cause was heart disease. Miss Randall, 81, had lived in North Bennington since 1987 and had been a strong advocate for the preservation of open space and other environmental causes.

Miss Randall's seven volumes of poetry won numerous national awards and recognition, including the 1987 Poet's Prize. In 1980, the American Poetry Society presented her the prestigious Percy Bysshe Shelley Award for her body of work. She also received grants from the National Endowment for the Arts, the National Institute of Arts and Letters and the Sewanee Review fellowship in poetry.

Though she maintained a quiet life, far from literary conferences and competitions, Randall won the friendship and respect of many of her peers, including such noted poets as the late Josephine Jacobsen and George Garrett, poet laureate of Virginia. The late Howard Nemerov, a Pulitzer Prize-winner and U.S. P[oet] Laureate, publicly of Randall's early

Returning to Baltimore Randall taught at Gouch[er]

A native of Baltimo[re] Miss Randall first moved [to Ver]mont in the 1940s, wh[en she] attended Bennington Coll[ege...] her, the college represen[ted] only an educational oppo[rtunity,] but a chance to rebel aga[inst] debutante balls and soci[ety] parties she had been ra[ised to] attend. Studies in literat[ure and] science led to a year at [Johns Hopkins] Medical School and to wo[rk as a] technician in the Harvard [medi]cal laboratory. In 195[0 she] received her master's de[gree in] English from Johns Hopk[ins and] embarked on a long ca[reer] teaching literature at the [college] level. In 1952, she marri[ed Philip] Sawyer, an art critic for Th[e Balti]more Sun. They moved t[o Boston] for a few years, during wh[ich she] taught at the University o[f Mary]land's overseas extensio[n...] couple's tiny coldwater flat [was the] site of frequent parties for [Ameri]can artists, including painte[rs Mark] Rothko and sculptor [Louis] Falkenstein.

# THE PATH TO FAIRVIEW

NEW AND SELECTED POEMS BY

## JULIA RANDALL

LOUISIANA STATE UNIVERSITY PRESS   BATON ROUGE AND LONDON   1992

Copyright © 1987, 1989, 1992 by Julia Randall
All rights reserved
Manufactured in the United States of America
First printing
01  00  99  98  97  96  95  94  93  92     5  4  3  2  1

DESIGNER: AMANDA MCDONALD KEY
TYPEFACE: SABON
TYPESETTER: G&S TYPESETTERS, INC.
PRINTER AND BINDER: THOMSON-SHORE, INC.

Library of Congress Cataloging-in-Publication Data

Randall, Julia, date.
  The path to Fairview : new and selected poems / by Julia Randall.
    p.   cm.
  ISBN 0-8071-1782-X (alk. paper). — ISBN 0-8071-1783-8 (pbk. : alk. paper)
  I. Title.
PS3535.A56274P38  1992
811'.54—dc20                                                          92-19003
                                                                          CIP

The poems herein have been selected from *The Solstice Tree* (Baltimore, 1952), copyright © 1952 by Mary Owings Miller, renewed 1980 by Julia Randall; *Mimic August* (Baltimore, 1960), copyright © 1960 by Mary Owings Miller, renewed 1988 by Julia Randall; *The Puritan Carpenter* (Raleigh, N.C., 1965), copyright © 1961, 1962, 1964, 1965 by Julia Randall; *Adam's Dream* (New York, 1969), copyright © 1966, 1967, 1968, 1969 by Julia Randall; *The Farewells* (Chicago, 1981), copyright © 1981 by Julia Randall; and *Moving in Memory* (Baton Rouge, 1987), copyright © 1984, 1985, 1986, 1987 by Julia Randall. Grateful acknowledgment is made to the editors of publications in which poems in this volume previously appeared, some in slightly different form: *American Poetry Review, American Scholar, Bennington Review, Botteghe Obscure, Contemporary Poetry, Gathering Voices, Hampden-Sydney Poetry Review, Hollins Critic, Hopkins Review, Imagi, Johns Hopkins Magazine, Lowlands Review, Maryland Poetry Review, Maxy's Journal, Nebo, Poetry, Provincial, Quarterly Review of Literature, Red Clay Reader, Sewanee Review, Southern Poetry Review, Southern Review, Tennessee Poetry Review, Vanderbilt Poetry Review,* and *Voices.* "Adam's Dream" was first published by the Tinker Press; "Charity Begins . . . ," "Two-Part Song," "Loving 1," "Singing Christmas," and "Hello, Betsy Parrish" first appeared in *The Hollins Poets,* published by the University Press of Virginia. "Video Games" is from the *Kenyon Review.* Of the new poems, "A Winter Gallery" is reprinted from *Chrysalis;* "Gone Missing," from the *Michigan Quarterly;* and "In Memory of Francis Fergusson, 1904–1986" and "Twenty-One Turkeys," from *Ploughshares.*

Publication of this book has been supported by a grant from the National Endowment for the Arts in Washington, D.C., a federal agency.

The paper in this book meets the guidelines for permanence and durability of the Committee on Production Guidelines for Book Longevity of the Council on Library Resources.∞

CONTENTS

FROM *THE SOLSTICE TREE* (1952)
 A Carolling 3
 The Leaking Library 3
 Local Weather 4

FROM *MIMIC AUGUST* (1960)
 Inscape I 9
 Inscape II 9
 Question: Of the Effects of Love 9
 Appalachian 10
 October 2 10
 October 3 11
 October 4 11
 In Absence of Music 12

FROM *THE PURITAN CARPENTER* (1965)
 Rockland 17
 The Man on the Parking Lot 17
 To William Wordsworth from Virginia 19
 A Scarlet Letter About Mary Magdalene 20
 Boundbrook 21
 The Farmer's Tale 22
 The Coast 23
 Maryland 24
 Maid's Song 26
 Science and Poetry: Three Comments 26
 For a Homecoming 27
 Miracles 28
 Stygian 28
 For T.R., 1908–1963 29
 Reviewing *The Tempest* for Midterms 30
 Variations: The Puritan Carpenter 31
 Figure 35
 Montmorency 35
 Advent Poems, 1963 37
 Danaë 40
 The Fool's Tongue 41
 A Trim Reckoning 42
 For a Going-Out 42
 Garden Set 43
 Suit 45
 The Winds 46

To William Wordsworth from Vermont 46
The Silo Under Angel's Gap 48
There Was a Bird 49
Cirque d'Hiver 50
A Ballad of Eve 50
The Seasons 51
A Journey 53
For Christmas, 1960 54

FROM *ADAM'S DREAM* (1969)
Tallis' Canon 59
1 Diurne 59
2 Nocturne 60
Blue 60
Two-Part Song 60
Charity Begins . . . 61
The Bennett Springs Road 62
Starlings 62
The Fascinating World of Fungi 63
The Writer Indulges a Hobby 64
On Not Getting the Phono Fixed 64
Mail 65
Insomnia 66
Legend 66
Loving 1 67
Loving 2 68
As Theory 68
Pietà: December 69
Letter 70
Histoire 71
Santa Maria delle Grazie 71
Adam's Dream 71
Singing Christmas 74
Xmas Shopping 75
Sans Day Carol 76
Derivative 77
Farmer Blake 78
A Meditation in Time of War 79
1 Jan 66 80
Falling Dead 81
Hello, Betsy Parrish 81
Sabbatical 82
Staying at Home 83
End of Leave 84

Ground Glass   85
Earth Science   85
The Ring   88
The Wall   89
Glimpses of the Moon   90
Da Capo   91

FROM *THE FAREWELLS* (1981)
  Departure   95
  The Sycamores at Satyr Hill   95
  Another Part of the County   96
  Naming the Gunpowder Falls   97
  Matchman   97
  Hardwood Country   98
  The Trackers   99
  Album Leaves   100
  Outliving   104
  Family Portraits   104
  Stratford, O.   106
  The Man Who Made a River   107
  Giverny   107
  R. van R.   108
  Cumae   108
  A Farewell to Music   109
  The Soloist   109
  Falling Asleep in Chapel   110
  Eve Enters Heaven   112
  A Child Enters Heaven   113
  The Blind Schoolmaster Enters Heaven   113
  A Puritan Enters Heaven   113
  A Mariner Enters Heaven   114
  The Prodigal Enters Heaven   114
  A Whole Man Enters Heaven   115
  Salvation Kit   115
  Degeneration   116
  Jill upon Love & Language   117
  The Bird That Sang Mozart   118
  Continuum   118
  Touchstones   119
  An Elegy of Sorts   120
  The White Rhinos   121
  The Kingfisher, February   121
  Arrival   122

FROM *MOVING IN MEMORY* (1987)
   Middle Age, Middle East   125
   The Clearing   125
   Thunder   127
   Grackles   128
   "Blooms All Summer"   128
   The Banana Tree at Carney   129
   Trumpet Vine   130
   Anthracnose   131
   Praying in Space   132
   The Wilderness of This World   133
   Dingman's Falls   134
   Duncansby Head   136
   Skara Brae   136
   Dun's Scotus's Carinish   137
   Tripping   137
   Rosa   138
   Second Childhood   139
   Adeste Fideles: Christmas, 1982   139
   Christmas, 1984   140
   Mysteries   141
   Video Games   142
   Homage to Corot   143
   Notes from Cézanne   144
   Arias   145
   Translation   147
   Silence   148
   Subtracted Memories   148
   Assorted Masters Perform   149
   For the Keeper of MSS   150
   Recipes   151
   The Economy, the Environment, etc.   152
   I Love New York, Virginia, Channel 2, Pier 1, etc.   152
   Cooking the Heart   153
   A Dream of Reunion   155
   Touchstones II   156
   Moving in Memory   158
   A Valediction   161

NEW POEMS
   Keeping Time   165
   Storm King   166
   Jan. 1, 1991   167
   September 1, 1990   167

A Book   168
Hamlet   169
Bedivere's Tale   169
Bedivere's Rhymes   171
Heimweh   174
Nearly Anon.   174
Hey Baxter   174
Twenty-One Turkeys   175
The Baptist Owls   176
Whitman's   176
The Ancient Ladies   177
In Memory of Francis Fergusson, 1904–1986   177
Becoming Nobody   178
To a Friend Dying   179
Gone Missing   180
Le Goût d'Ailleurs   181
Lots for Sale   181
Yellowstone Burning   182
Love at Last Sight   183
To W.B.Y.   183
Gray's Anatomy   184
A Winter Gallery   185

FROM *THE SOLSTICE TREE* (1952)

## A Carolling

When winter was
Fabled with fires,
It was angels, angels,
Sang to the cold stars.

Berry and thorn they sang,
Shepherd and beast,
Stranger to haven come,
And homing ships.

Who tells a color?
Fennel and rose
That sprang in winter
From the crippled ice.

Who tells my true love?
For the heart's cold
That sought a stranger's son
Low to the world.

When winter comes
And snow to wear,
Make we our solstice tree
Of the dark fir.

And candled, kindled,
Famous with stars,
Our solemn season show
Song to the new years.


## The Leaking Library

Or an exhibition
of wet books. So, fanned out
from courteous spines, in deepened hues, to dry
across the summer-bare reserve shelves, they
deploy in sudden space before our eyes,
red coats, buff coats, blue coats. And they are ours
in odd expansions: mountain, desert, lake,
acre or fabled continent our sights
assume, they travel. Where we gaze, they strike
from every eye. We are the space they take.

These rags, this dye—
what syllable did the accurate rain
assemble, what scored note
the hurricane detach? Vermont's wild throat
I shouted in, a child, and shouted out
of civil pages, lending to the sun
what candles from the gentle dead had won.
These have no voices: bellflower, granite, pool
where the killdeer watches, wind on the cricket hill.
We are the concert, we of breath entire
perform illiterate June from an inky score.

If here
under the hammer's ring at the roofing, we
confer gold Helen with an instant tower,
she must not mourn. We burn
total as Troy. The Odyssey in the eye,
with the curled Greek, contracts to history.
The buckram dress, the carbon character
own summer with its hill, its minstrel tongue
all stationed, all unstrung. But in these still
ranks of the ranging pages, not the flood
that quenched a hundred villages could stain
a tress, a rampart. Troy will sail again
to Carthage, and to Latium, as we come
here to a hospitable shore, and learn
time's gift, the habit of completion.


## Local Weather

It is a quiet winter here.
Olive and gray and touched with sun,
Our fallows and our woods appear
Themselves; December's dun
Invites the gaudy jay, his scree
Scatters the small birds from their bread.
The lake will freeze. Occasionally
It snows, but never hard
Enough to smooth the hollows out
Or hunch the rusty privet up.

But we, as if we cracked at heart,
Cry up some shaggy bourne of ice

Where mirrors bluer than our skies
Repeat the useless canisters
Of gin and pemmican and pills.
We shout. Our voices snowball back
Too softly from the glacier's walls
And, freezing in our furs, we die
A phantom, television death.

Dear friends, if New Year has a wish,
I pray you draw no polar breath
In some imported wilderness.
These thirty years and more I track
A path across our natural state
Where metaphorical distress
Screams random over every gate
To hide the family mess within.

I pray the weathers of our blood
Be temperate, and we invent
Domestic measures for the flood
Of need, the leak of turpitude,
The snowy feathers of our dream.
We can do what the weatherman,
With all his dials and needles, can't:
We can be what, occasionally, we seem.

From *Mimic August* (1960)

## Inscape I

Between the fever and the stone,
the nerve's kick and the clay's condition

only with sight time lightens, only
with beetles under the leaves, and leaves

ripped from the seabranch. So the shape
compels attention at the eye,

so is the hour outdone. Sing low
the dagger in his living. You

that curl the blind hand over the breast,
sing for a sign, sign for a feast,

fasten the blade, explore the vein,
learn the familiar blood.


## Inscape II

Unlock my tongue the lily stone
the seajaw's pebble subtly laid

strange note strange song dragged up the tide
strange syllable but still your own

as still your own dragged down the sky
the mad the miracle-wreaking moon

october's cry. The mood resounds
from pale to flame, from flame to ice

the mood resounds, the mood recites
walls, wombs, and seasons in its dress

the water that the hand unwinds
the tears of its own face.


## Question: Of the Effects of Love

Aquin, thy servant in the tongue
to sip the honey, justice, tell
proportion, recommend the strong

to a strong course, perfection's—thus
ranging, in time, perfection's match:
union, indwelling, ecstasy
in every love, as mirrors each of each.

But question, sir, in simpler parts
offered as brimming to the event,
superfluous origins: the sad
defections of the final sweet;
question image to image set
as signature to arts of grace;
hold being, for glory, to a loss
dead to the subtlest school's exploit.

## Appalachian

Light on these leaves November makes
that was a yellow year your face,
Hyannis, Truro, and the house
needlequick, seaspoiled, moors a piece.

As seasonless as sands must keep
I in this gold mosaic care
to send sight only, only sight,
after the southward drift of things.

Who with her closer heart would dare
commit the falling of that fire
perform the brute historian?

The thicket history of wings
November makes, and ashes own
the sycamore's decline from green.

## October 2

My proctoring stones show riot raw:
how else, rock heart, were we to know
riot was not prerogative
of this flushed corporal creature, love?

How limbs would lie in deep delight
of plumage, granite sets at nought;

chalk looms a constant quietude
on wild occasions of the blood.

Oh blaze and quake! more phantom shows,
dearer than every self that is
no child of seasons, what rock hand
fashioned me its aspiring friend?

## October 3

This shear of things shows sooner stars:
how space we thought compacted bore
above that chamber of the year
vaults to make sweet the dust of years.

Speech hangs in heaven, as then, by day,
speech clung upon the grass to stay,
and held the locust only gold,
and in its shade love's shape the world.

How shall our eyes enlarge and keep
us, in this vaster weather, wed?
hearts whom the narrow summer hid
in thickest joy, in greenest hope.

Ribbed things, rock colors of the source
of softness, mark the landscape out:
now shall we fix ourselves in this,
bare, but remembering softnesses;

part, but accounted; wide, but set
where summer in all her leaves was hit
and we from one another's space
stared on the sudden universe.

## October 4

Colors a continent away
from granite-borne Tuolumne
call out our blood, sudden as pain
between two lethargies

                       (ah dream,
soft-headed summer, sealing hot

our honey-suckled lips on quiet!
dream, dream, December, of the sap
crystalled fantastic in some deep
secreted chamber against light).

Sudden as shock, cry pierced to bone
at waking birth, these hills describe
crimson our quickness, shaken out
an instant, while the maples burn.

Sierra, now to insight rise
mountains of fire, mountains of ice:
the odd contractions of the core
that cast you, and the sheets that wore
the weather of an age on rock.

Our paltry weather falls and goes,
reminderless, where ages sleep,
ephemeral as the nights and days
beneath whose scattering breath you keep
what cold contortions shape our praise.

Tahoe, Tehama, now our eyes,
awaking west, beneath your names
find the perdurable hills at last
of passion molded in the forms.


## In Absence of Music

Here, maple-pressed, elm-pressed, the lead noon shade
anchors the catbirds' squabble, fixes the eye
of the observer of catbirds, yet not as named
in that relation, not as any name
but undershade, consubstance, spiky green,
fair quiet of the spiky spirit's clay.

It is one direction: Thyrsis as Arcady:
the midge, the rill, the rye, the blood, the bone,
composed in touch, a metabolic peace.

Yet to desire a more precise relief,
a portrait I of parts, more finely etched,
as: the observer of catbirds in blue canvas shoes
in dry-ditch August at high, peasant noon
under the eaten east-side elm: that man.

Yet to derive him? clap the limiting tongue
on its large communions? Aid us, ordering time,
as if the sun departed—

As if, Domenico, your sudden scale
scattered the silence of meridian
into its proper throats: dumb air, stiff tree,
surfeited bird, most inarticulate Tom;
as if the notes disposed the substance: fugue:
fixing the corners of a formal now
in which, by means of which, though once, we live.

FROM *THE PURITAN CARPENTER* (1965)

# Rockland

Masters, be kind to the old house that must fall,
Burn, or be bulldozed. The apples have grown small
And the ivy great here. The walk must be moved once more
Beyond the holly. Do not use the side door,
The lilies have broken the step. If you fix it,
They will break it again; they live under the stone.
There is blown glass
In three windows; hold them up with a stick.
The smoke is always thick
With the first fire. The Landseer in the attic
Was tacked there when I came. There is a snake
With a red tongue in the terrace; he has never been known
To hurt. The worst leak
Is in the bedroom ceiling. So. It was a good house
For hands to patch, a boon to August eyes. And when
The moon lay on the locusts, and the stream
Croaked in the bottom, muted by high grass,
Small rustlings in the woodlot, birdcries, was
A minister like music. Should I say
This—with the apple tree—was Sirmio,
This—with the two-year parsley—Twickenham,
Aldworth, or Abbotsford, I would only mean
We lease one house in love's divided name.


# The Man on the Parking Lot

The man on the parking lot
Is some sort of cripple, not
That he limps or hasn't his eyes:
I know when I hear his voice
Cry, Lady! Lady! with more
Urgency than the police.
It is hoarse like a dog with rage
Against my human shape.
I roll the window up
Instinctively; he is right
There, snarling at the glass.
This week, like the week before,
I am in the wrong space.

I am only going to buy
Beer. It is Saturday.
They have locked the Union Trust;
The lot is virtually empty.
But which is Robinson's spot?
It didn't rain in September;
Then it was by the door.
All the sloppy weather
It was about as far
Away as you could get
By the uncleared exit.
Now he is screaming me down
To the Battery Service wall.
There has never been a sign.

He has an ugly will
This Cerberus. I accept
The scutcheons of the Law
Which shine for all to see:
The traffic must move smoothly.
Take Martin Chenowith.
I had at least three tickets
From him in the mythic past.
In fear of God and Father
I scrounged five dollars from
My small, unlicensed brother
And took it humbly in
To the station-house in person,
Grateful that I could pay
For silence and regulation.
Now the old eagle bows
To me, at my moneyed house,
Where he keeps the swinging door,
Un-uniformed, old, poor,
But kind as he always was
Behind the imposing laws.

I do not seek excuse.
I could give up beer,
Or change my liquor store.
I could lock the car
And leave it. I could force
The dog of the Union Trust
To his superiors.
I could make endless wars.

And yet, and yet
It moves me like a game,
Though I have never been right,
And sometimes my teeth are set
All the way home
In anger or fear or both;
Though the monstrous guardian
Pursues me in a dream
Around the drive-in booth.
Does he keep the vaulted dead?
Am I seeking to get in
Or stay out? How do I win?
I have certainly missed my slot.

But next and next week, led
By rote, or temerity,
It will be Lady! Lady!
Lady! around the lot
Where I will never fit.

The mongrel lies at ready.
My Sunday beer is sweet.


# To William Wordsworth
# from Virginia

I think, old bone, the world's not with us much.
I think it is too difficult to see,
But easy to discuss. Behold the bush.
His seasons out-maneuver Proteus.
This year, because of the drought, the barberry
Is all goldflakes in August, but I'll still say
To the First Grade next month, "*Now* it is Fall.
You see the leaves go bright, and then go small.
You see October's greatcoat. It is gold.
It will lie on the earth to keep the seed's foot warm.
Then, Andrew Obenchain, what happens in June?"
And Andrew, being mountain-bred, will know
Catawba runs too deep for the bus to get
Across the ford—at least it did last May,
And school was out, and the laundry wouldn't dry,
And when the creek went down, the bluebells lay
In Hancock's pasture-border, thick as hay.

What do they tell the First Grade in Peru,
I wonder? All the story: God is good,
He counts the children, and the sparrow's wing.
God loved William Wordsworth in the spring.
William Wordsworth had enough to eat.
Wye was his broth, Helvellyn was his meat,
And English was his cookstove. And where did words
Come from, Carlyle Rucker? Words that slide
The world together. Words that split the tide
Apart for Moses (not for Mahon's bus),
Words that say, the bushes burn for us—
Lilac, forsythia, orange, Sharon rose—
For us the seasons wheel, the lovers wait,
All things become the flesh of our delight,
The evidence of our wishes.

       Witch, so might
I stand beside the barberry and dream
Wisdom to babes, and health to beggar men,
And help to David hunting in the hills
The Appalachian fox. By words, I might.
But, sir, I am tired of living in a lake
Among the watery weeds and weedy blue
Shadows of flowers that Hancock never grew.
I am tired of my wet wishes, of running away
Like all the nymphs, from the droughty eye of day.
Run, Daphne. Run, Europa, Io, run!
There is not a god left underneath the sun
To balk, to ride, to suffer, to obey.
Here is the unseasonable barberry.
Here is the black face of a child in need.
Here is the bloody figure of a man.
Run, Great Excursioner. Run if you can.


## A Scarlet Letter About Mary Magdalene

If I asked you to look out
The back window, where the crumbs are spread,
And asked you who was king
Of the sparrows, you would say the red
Bird, not a sparrow, and not because

He has manners, or is larger than them all.
He is not more virtuous:
He is more beautiful.

It is hard to conceive
A god irrational as man,
But we believe
In the image, patch it as we can.
We fall in love
Not with the best or brightest in the nest
Of reason, but some light in the heart's cave.

And that, perhaps, my dear, is how we save
Ourselves. How after a life of sin,
We say, "I love you," and we enter in
Unworthy, to the kingdom which he made,
Where weak are strong, whores maid,
And oily love announces: I obeyed
Necessity, who blessed me.
God possessed me.


## BOUNDBROOK

I met a man and he was fair.
All the birds said Follow.
Every leaf in the wood
Shook gold onto my head
And my heart felt all its blood.

Then it was a great park land
By a willow-trailing brook bound round.
Stag and peacock walked
For pleasure in the corn,
And Merlin wound the horn.

Merlin or his tribe it was
Spun that park and lordly palace
Pearled as Helen's pin.
My master said, Walk in,
And, Touch me. It is yours.

I had a hand could change a world.
The waters dropped, the meadow furled,
That field was Circe's pen.

The shaggy beasts growled at the shucks,
Great swine, and goats, and picking cocks,
And they were all my kin.

Seven years I sojourned there,
The blacksnake nested in the briar,
Every bird was black.
Insects stained the air like smoke.
I struck and ravined in the thick
Until my heart's blood broke.

And I lay down, a beast, to die
And rose up seven years ago
In the poplar fields of home.
There the streams go out and in,
All the men are common men,
The blackbird whistles in the corn.
Touch me. It is mine.


## The Farmer's Tale

Farmer, farmer, tell me,
My crop is slow to make,
Your wagon goes to market
Seven days a week.

You've melon for your daughter
And berry for your son.
Now by the rain that falls the same,
Why have I none?

Because the rain is equal,
Because the seed is true,
It is not every husbandman
His pulse and pastures grow.

Who sows a marble acre
Six of his seeds will die,
Let him hoe and shelter,
Let him weep and pray,

Let him shield the seventh,
Though market be there none,
Neither maize nor melon,
Neither daughter nor son.

There comes a lusty flower,
But rare, rare.
I cannot tell the color
But people at the Fair

Recall a ruined farmer
Who danced upon a stone
Until it bore that wonder,
The glory of the town,

The envy of the country.
But none could buy that bloom.
He flung it to the farmer's boy
And struck up harvest home.


## THE COAST

How, arriving from any waste,
The heart leaps to the guiding coast.
Without the eyes' assurance
Even our instruments and natural talents
Are poor props in the random troughs
Of hills and waters. Crest on crest,
Planet on planet tries the chart of space.
Even savage rocks,
After plains passed or surf run,
Miles of the sluggish river, years of stars,
Even the rocks' rude direction
Settles our task. There will be dunes to cross,
Cliffs, entering bays. But north, south, east, or west,
Their line sets out a continent, bounds a home
For inland exploration.

                            May I return,
Thus, from the wilds of absence, where I lose
Feature, being one with all the elements,
Wave with the drifted wave, or light in air,
Blown seed with seed, straight to the edge and center
Of all my maps, my saving break in space,
My love: not Caribee to Columbus
Gives better name, or locates wandering faith
More sure than the wished-for dangers of your face.

## Maryland

True, there are other places more
Comfortable for the climate. If one lives
By one's skin, there is always California. By one's eye,
An Alp, or the distant prospect of the Bay
Of Salerno from the Belvedere
Cimbrone (where one can also die
Of the heat). But it is not that. One takes
The sun as it comes (provided it comes)
Quite naturally. There are fans,
Swimming pools, sprinklers, screens, and bug
Bombs. Even the sycamore
Has been known to stir, and locust in August storms
Cracks. As one takes
Sumac, ailanthus, mulberries on the sill,
The cornflower, the whippoorwill (this is the first year
I have seen an oriole south of New Jersey),
Tomatoes and tobacco. Not one rare
Peculiar thing, except the Naval Academy, or the great
Dilapidated hospital: Come to me,
Ye disconsolate foreign princes, blue babies from
Georgia, and Bill and Van,
Every Saturday night, from Wolfe Street. And I will give you
Pigeons, watermelon, Edgar Allan
Poe, the Star Spangled
Banner,
And the Carrolls, Howards, Ridgelys, Warfields, Blairs,
Whose beaming swords were turned into ploughshares,
First, then Georgian mansions, and gray stone farms
For the younger brothers; now for all, for all,
The golf course, the shopping center, and the Foxhall
Homes of distinction. As if every village
Did not have heroes, born, adopted, dead,
Buried, or partially buried (when the head
And heart lived separate). You are approaching
Hillsboro, New Hampshire, the birthplace
Of President Franklin Pierce. And in the ex-Convento,
Amalfi, the lettered memory of
Enrico Wadsworth Longfellow, very far
From Gitchee-Gumee, and the styles of snow
On Brattle Street.

No, it is not the local habitation—
Cedars by whitewashed fences, some half gone

With honeysuckle. And not Chesapeake, the name.
No, it is knowing them somehow for one's own,
Environs of the single history
That matters, and a force in it. Thus,
One could wear sneakers on the rue de
Rivoli, but never on Charles Street, for they look,
Those doctors' offices, and those sad apartments,
The Sheraton-Belvedere, and those purveyors
Of reproduction antique furniture,
They look with Grandmother's eyes, and they carry the news
Home to one's conscience. Or say that one should meet
Mrs. Lenhart in Cleveland. One would say, "How dull,"
And be right. But in the A & P
At Roland and Deepdene, one somehow remembers
Those who were nice to Father, those who sent
A bouquet at graduation, those whose sons
Are missing since Korea, those who fix
Clocks, those who know the recipe
For cucumber aspic.

Somewhere, Sir Thomas Browne,
In a friend's face, dying, saw a ghost of bone
Rise, and the family feature
Clear off the curves of earned, familiar nature:
Lusts, comforts, every lineament of school,
Or private light of industry or travel.
Pure Peter vanished, and the patient lay
Pure Willoughby, pure Cameron, family clay
Startled to reclamation. Then if place,
Too, is our ancestor (that is
The forever England concept), this low east,
Like love, rides in the gesture of my flesh.
Green Appalachian must outlast
Apennine or Sierra—even the sun
That struck on Shasta while we ate
Lunch, and the hoary marmots watched, or even
Dust on that mountain steeper than the way
From Lerici to Turbia. Cardinal
Cannot turn nightingale, wisteria come
Hawthorn or oleander, nor I root
Far from Patapsco's ledges, or Wye's foot.

## Maid's Song

I wept on cypress knees,
I made a coat of moss,
I took the glowing worm
And hid him from the grass.

The river moved but once,
I could not plant my foot,
I'd mouths about my arm.
At last my love went out.


## Science and Poetry: Three Comments

1
To grate the greenness of the green
Is not, mynheer, to desecrate
The grail of crusted artistry
Whose fictive emeralds wink as bright.

We two set forth from Camelot:
The analytic with his board
To bare the essential animal,
And you, my unaccoutred bard,
Describing sounds of hoo and ha,
And jigging at resemblances.

Our strategies, mynheer, diverge,
But Joseph keeps the chapel warm,
And curious questers up and down
Spy out the samite mysteries.

Record, doktor. And fool, jig on.

2
The moon that was our mystery
Is that pocked orb and weary ash.

But who, careening in borrowed light,
Questions the cinder's potency?

As if the new geography
Were parenthetic to our scheme—

As if, occasionally, one caught
Echoes of actual Artemis.

3
There is no limiting of the blue
That leaps above the blue beyond.
There is the unwillingness to look
Over the frosty burdock's head
In this December floor of light.

In this December floor of light
As if the shimmering twig were all,
And dull that pierceless cupola.

So dull that pierceless cupola,
Imagination flaked beneath:
As if the gods themselves were cast
In moods of ours to icy death.


## For a Homecoming

I wish you were not flying, and I wish
Women were not fond, and men were not foolish.
Who'd ever invent
Wings out of wax, that had godsent
Patience-plumes to plumb her element?
Safe in my space, and surfeited, I stare
At the new violence in the air,
And think of little boys who screw the tops
Off the cleaning fluid, and knot the heads of mops,
And peel the bark off trees, and kick the stones
When there's no one around to pester with questions.
Oh, I know,
I'd be content in a cave, and I know that some
Incredibly curious germ of evolution
Lets you conceive a rafter and a beam
And a plastic tablecloth. A single name
Is all my woe, whatever was first on the tongue
In the beginning. Disaster and joy came then
Honestly: a banana was not a storm,
Absent was over, present was, possibly, warm.
But oh the daisy-petal words: is not,
Is or is not, is safe, tired, hungry, sick,
Unfaithful, lost, laughing, will not come home,
Will come home late. I will not sleep all night,
Preparing the news, hearing the morning break

In the trees, and the wings unfold that cannot make
Any but natural journeys while they wake.


## MIRACLES

I said to the stream, Be still, and it was still.
I walked across the water like a fool.
Such ease—you'd think a man had never tried
The simple miracles, but lived and died
Sweating at wood and steel: chop, forge, bend, bind,
Get up the armory, don't trust humankind,
They were damned from the start.
                              I said to the mineral hill,
Lie down, and the hanging rocks and the canyons fell
As soft as smoke. It was quiet. I called out
Some friends to look. For a while they walked about
Uncomfortably, I thought, and one picked up
A fragment for the Museum. Envy? Fear?
I don't know what. I kept on all that year.
Wherever I went, the trees bowed down; the fruit
Rolled like obedient coins to my feet,
And so on. Late one night I tried to command—
How shall I say?—my holy spell to end,
Break, blast, unmagic me here in the dark
Tower I'd built. I wanted a horn to knock
The cullis in, and the crazy ditch to rise.
Oh God, for the need of nails, for the wild eyes
Of Noah with creation in his hold
Stampeding. But I'd sold
My Ararat for meadows. Oh, the flowers!
Too deep, too deep.
I said, accept my tears.


## STYGIAN

I had heard in my youth
Of the water that bound the earth
Like a supple, fatal beast
With his tail in his mouth,
Immense and circular.

I never stopped to fear
The little bending creeks,
Susquehanna's arcs,
Or the turns of Delaware,
Till last night when I came
To the ford at Coldstone Gap.
I saw a serpent's eye
Glint in the running light,
And held one foot in the air
And one on the crossing rock.
Something was dead on the shore.
I did not stop to look
But took Catawba's wall
And shouted coming over
To Craig and Newcastle,
"I have crossed the world's river!"


## For T.R., 1908–1963

Lurcher from Genesis, long man of light,
Maker past making, beggar crippled back
Past crying alms of earth or alms of air,
I cannot reach you in the near field where
Your cells ungather darkly on their ways
To mine and bloom and all the million bodies
Time chances for the homing of its play.
The nameless need no comfort; it is we
Cry brother, brother to the witless grass,
And ghostly from the flesh of all that was
The first voice sings that turned the deep to day.

When monstrous and unorthodox you lay
Mouth open to the moss and called it kin,
Unearthed the crooked meat beneath the stone,
Went fishways, eyed the breather in the slime,
Or up, sat up not hay-high in your fur
To stop the vireo and freeze the weather,
All kind religions faltered. What is man
If his chief good and market in his time
Is feeding lips and bones dropped down to root?
You said, time was before my bones stood up,
Time was before my tongue, formed in the dark,
Sang him together for a dwelling-place.

His pyramids of sleepers are my house,
His planets are the fire-fields where I walk
Befriended into waking.

                          Journeyman,
Come ride me now a little into green,
You and your company. In my low air
A patient music moves, as of the light
Gathered in leaves, and I, a gatherer
Of void intimations, make this shape
For you to live in, and I know not what
Children to cradle shell-like at their ear.
It's blood alone, the wise men say, they hear.

Loud blood it is, and running on the bone,
Builds griefs and muscled pleasures of its own,
But secret brings the sea, secret the land
Limned out for love, where every bone shall stand
Stiff in the fellowship of the first word
That spoke man, mineral, petal, minnow, bird.


## Reviewing *The Tempest* for Midterms

My Ariel sings like Haydn.
Prosper me, good grace.
I am all loss
Now, in this island of my winter house,
Son, brother, lover dreamed of, done.
The moon looks out as never a storm
Had bruised her blind, unmagicked eye.
The telltale snow
Shows ghastlier now.

How many fathoms fell the rain?
Will that music come again?
The queen my mother drowned before.
I know the taste of sea-water.

Sweet guide, restore my neighborhood
With day. Make all dreams fade,
Especially the good. I had once pearl eyes
And coral bones and sea-cut palaces.
But Ariel, Ariel, I could not kiss!

## Variations: The Puritan Carpenter

1

I gave my love a scarlet cloak,
But dun he dyed it, skirt and yoke.
I gave my love a dancing tune,
But he went marching on and on.

I gave my love a world to live
Without a gibbet or a grave,
But such a carpenter was he,
He built the coffin and the tree.

2

I do not dance, I do not sing.
Quiet on a weekday morning,
With a candle and a broom
I set to rights my single room:
Rind to larder, rug to bed,
Book to time, and dream to need.

I do not run, I do not stop.
The compass of my hall is sweet:
Log to winter, air to May.
Even years spare me and serve me.

    Strawblood, dancing on a line,
    Have you passions of your own?

3

I too have built a house,
Muscle and nerve and bone
Gray as mason's dust,
Have fitted mortar and stone,
Fitted stone and mortar
Against the plunging moon
And her bitter weather.

Any port from storm,
Fortress or pleasure-dome
Over the caves of ice
Or the sacred river.
Who takes the raging sun?
None, since Adam's eye

Looked naked on his own
Bald and staining body.

I shall be dressed to die.

4
Come, build a cage for the mind,
Set it water and meat,
That else would rage through the night
With honey and gall to eat,
And bruise its travelling feet
On the mountain-tracks of desire:
Wind's horn, rock's spine,
Rain's cup, October's tinder.

I count a little square,
Pallet and hewn trough,
Where the light comes quiet,
World enough, world enough.

5
Keep the hawk blind,
Keep the dog chained.
The limb unleashed
And the unleashed mind
Grow tame and easy,
Easy and tame
Learning the wind
That shifts the sun
From crag to lawn,
Lawn to tree,
Over and over again
Learning the small rain.
But for the war
On the trespasser
Of earth or air,
For the clean kill
At the nerve's edge
And the belly full,
Keep the eye down
From comfort, fierce
From the brain's caul,
From the blood's noose.

6
You will never trace me
In the bedevilled dew.

Cloak and staff in my entry
Summer and winter through
Hang well-pegged. For the Hangman
Will come. I shall be ready,
Booted and brushed, still new
For my wedding journey.

7

If you should force my entry
In the night,
And crack against my posts, groping for light,
And pain of light sprung on the feeling blind,
I did not deal the murder. Like your kind,
You magicked in the old spell of the moon,
Poor lanterned worm, that could not light to bed
A millet grain. You kindled and you bled
Of that false fire, the cinder in the seed.
Make me no cry.
You ran upon the dagger. You will die.

8

Be strict, my dear, and stony,
And lock away my sins,
And you shall have a peaceful house
And quiet for your pains.

There is a peace of marble things,
Noble head and eye,
Mountainous, maybe—Everest,
Each of his seasons snow.

And then the dearer innocence:
Cold acres come to corn,
Such unpretentious monuments
As common pilgrims earn.

9

Before the frost has eaten
The crude remaining berry,
Fools see May in the tree
And the jewelled horn of plenty.

I have seen the hearts climb
Like crazy saps, and hang,
Trinkets of a season,
Until they are culled, flung,
Parched, consumed, or rotten;

Every sun the same
Rinse of gaudy hope.

Of cypress heart I made
Bench, table, and bed,
A floor to cripple the root,
A wall too smooth to suck,
And a roof to keep the shade.

In a room without a pulse
I practice for my peace.

## 10
I temper as I would
The seasons of my voice,
Make dew of iron rust,
And jessamine of ice.

I say I will not bear
August her sheaf, September
Her vine; rather among
Gravels go barren.

Unlearned of all heat,
Like stones, without a root
Or turgid stem, I sing
Against false spring.

## 11
High over the sea town,
Stone against the sky:
Shut love in a dark tower,
Love will die.

Like a child by the seashore,
I am foolish grown
Raising wall and turret
To watch them drown.

Mine is a sandy spirit,
Incapable of iron.

## 12
Farewell my love, and well my love
To sweep your garden clean,
For dock and crab grow thickest
Where marigolds have been.

Gravel your plot, and contemplate
An oriental span.
Rock is its own magnificence;
I keep my armor green.

## Figure

Light has no shape, but as it falls
Now on the mulberry, now on the rose,
Or creeps on grass.
Dark has no danger, but it takes
The depth of water, or the rock's
Plunge or foot-place.
So I move
To take some figure, or dissolve
Some face, some limb in shapeless love.
But you, by reason,
Bold as a winter oak, mark out
Acre and entranceway, and make
Shape of the season.

## Montmorency

When that July, unlike most threatened flames,
Descends in sheer magnificence of corn
Tongues, and the tiger lily's eyes
Answer the rude stare of the cyclops sun,
Then mariners, cool in the cave of dusk,
Survey these acres that the moony mist
Cannot disguise the care of, for the six
Spaced willows in the meadow wet their hair
Precisely where the guided brook sends up
Its silver, and this cedar points the air
Above the tables and the serenade
Like Vincent's trees, that lit the lamps of God.

But we concentrate
On the bugproof candles, now that dinner's gone
To be scraped for the dogs, behind the old facade.
Shall I tell you the horrid thing that Oggie said
When we went to camp? Remember it was

A thousand miles, the taxi after the plane
To Chester, and a dreadful price, I thought,
For that unupholstered jitney, especially when
He fishes half a day for his real living.
Well, anyway, we had to go in a boat
To see the senior life-saving, and Bart
Naturally took his shirt off; it wasn't hot
But there's not much sun in Canada, mostly fog,
Even inland. And do you know what
That child said, practically choking it out to me?
He said, "Please tell Daddy
To put his shirt back on."

Oh, do you raise
Terriers? I never buy a bitch
That doesn't have ten tits. I count them.

Yes, sometimes I pick up a book, but really
In winter it's the car pool every other
Week, and now that Tom is in New York
Three days, it's hard to organize my time.
I drink, much of the night, and go south
In the winter. One could hardly call it waste.
The rain-crow has retired. The nightingale
Does not visit our shores. Out in the years of space
What unnamed birds call music to our lips?
Oh I could speak and die to name one thing
In nature with an accurate name. The ships
Of our salvation throb. Put on your shirt,
Barton. Your hairs will wither at the root,
And all the race step forth as smooth as saints
In danger, or in love with God's own fire
That sings along the gables of this pyre.

# Advent Poems, 1963

> The shepherd's brow, fronting forked lightning, owns
> The horror and the havoc and the glory
> Of it.
> —G. M. Hopkins

1

I saw havoc strike a tree,
And where it fell, a dead man lay.
I saw sick stars and empires all
Shrivel to spots upon a pall.

I heard ghosts breed, and women crack.
The fur flew off the shepherd's back.
He crept on freezing knees to retch
Where naked kings stuck in a ditch.

I grew gigantic eyes to stare
Upon a shrinking insect's bier.
I pulled the knife out of my side,
And ashes greased the floors like blood.

2

Was this a dream? I left that house
At midnight where the murder was,
And crept on freezing knees to pray
To silence at the blackened tree.
But it grew blacker by my stare,
And burned away my eyes like fire,
And burned the pleasure from my loins,
And labor from my working arms,
And every cry my cold lips sent
Fell down in cinders. And I bent
Where all my guttering treasure lay,
And learned a second way to die.

3

It is silent under the steeple, cold enough
To crystallize the little light. The dead
Would tremble at that sign: one star, one note.
The stone could melt, the tree leaf: they do not.

The shroud of mourning coats me like a ghost,
And like a ghost, bone white, I gleam and sing

The folly of warmth and song, and of love most,
And the folly of grave comforting.

I came alone by light into this dark.
I laid the light like tears upon this stone,
Come late, come last to the bitter and difficult
Task: lay all things down.

I laid them all but what I could not spend,
The love that blood created in its lust
For love: my father's feature, the child-hymned
Warm breast, bright wing, one germ alone untarnished
In all that holocaust, one bone to cry.
What shall I cry? I burn in hell? And he:
I burn my child to honor, lest I die.

4
There is a worse than nothing: loose
The lewd mind from its bloody sheath
And let it plunder heaven and hell,
It cannot bid itself farewell
Until it creep under its skin
And hold its gibbering breath, and drown.

5
And the glory
Of it? That we will not die?
I walked the orchard in a winter thaw.
The ugly mud turned worms up to the sun,
And stiff mice softened for the harrier's maw.
Oh sparkling boughs! What is not animal
Breaks clean, or burns, or blooms without a will.
Without a will, it startles underground.
Without a will, it crackles in the sky.
Could my heart hear the Appalachian
Dull thunder break, if I lay still as stone
Under Catawba, still as poplar roots?
Still as this branch that stood the pruners' hooks?
Wind hones. Star sharpens. Now it is the time
Our peace, they say, stood up to bear our pain.
I lie down dusty. Father of seed and dream,
And if of mercy, bear me man again.

6
I walked the wild hills in the still of the year;
No blood but mine beat summer to its eye.

No eye but mine built Blue Ridge from the sea,
Or saw rough Tinker shudder and lie plain.

I have learned my history like other men,
Cracking the ice to see the water move,
Threading the thick brush grown upon the fire,
Conjuring love by all the names of time.

Conjuring one, the Child born over and over,
To be the secret name for the oak's shelter,
The secret name for the hawk's cross in the fur,
The winter rose, the parching head of summer.

In that sweet manger, darkened by the blood
Of beasts and innocent victims of his name,
Did God lie once, to suffer and be born
And weatherbit, under his vane of time?

The hare that has no wishes does not see
The Christmas angels breaking on my eye,
Or Easter wings performing feats of light.
I walk December in the dark and bright
Woods, and I wish, and see no more than he.

7

And who shall walk the tides of time
And lift the gates of Paradise?
One with swords upon his tongue
Or one with lilies in his eyes?

A heavy blade lay in a tree.
The legend ran: "Who takes me up
Shall fear no other enemy.
I cut the death-worm from the crop.

I spear the moth, I shave the rust.
I scatter every sandy house.
I flatten all the heads of lust.
I blind the little eyes of grass."

A child who could not read came by
And laid his hand upon my hand.
Inseparable, then and now,
We walked away across that land,

And begged at many a battened door,
And sang at many a sun-go-down,

Slept once on sand, and once on flower,
And finally, upon a tomb,

I traced this legend: Season me,
Thou Lord who counts the sparrow's quill.
Raise me in time bloom, bird, or tree,
Unsevered from my blood, thy will.

8
This was a dream. I drew that sword,
A feather, from the airy wood,
And walked with peace in all my blood.

The grass stood up along my way
The hawk, with pity in his eye,
Fed, phoenix-like, upon his prey.

This was the sword that cut the dream
Of self, the knife at my birth-string.
By blood alone I walk in time,
Weeping and praising.

9
Now burn, new born in winter's bin,
The hard moon and the stars between
Her rise above the orchard close
And set on Appalachian.

I see at morning with my tears
Burning the pruned and sparkling boughs,
From name to night, from flame to ice,
How little is her turning space.

Oh may this child new born, now burn
The arc of winter with her name,
Night's crescent, and returning day's
White shadow in her lifting eyes.


## Danaë

This love I make
Alone, and for my sake,
In a room of the summer town
Where you have never been.
I call his name a god,
His shape gold;

Since the sun cannot fall,
He comes glittering small,
Coining the air bright;
Finches in flight
He may be, or the great
Acacia falling over me.
I am laved
In radiance, each sense clean,
Loud awake in the dream
Where at last I know my name
Is Danaë, Danaë.

Oh when you speak that name,
My love, or one day when the little son
Crawls on his mother's breast, and I cannot tell
Myself from Rachel or Anna at the well,
One day when I chatter over my chores
And the light is late,
If there is a sudden glint
In my eyes, or a softening
Of habit-hard attendance, it is no soft dream,
But that by which I love you, and I am.

## The Fool's Tongue

"Tongue, hold! Tongue, hold!" I cried,
And when it would not stop
Raving upon it luck,
I told them how it lied.

From cellar to rooftop,
As it were not my own,
It turned my treasure up,
It knocked my treasure down.

And people came to steal
The coin of such a fool,
And laughed him off the land
With his lying tongue in his hand.

Till wandering by a grave
He cast the traitor in,
And though it could not rave,
Look how the travelling worm

Partook its mysteries,
Till he heard the small birds call
With his own voice from the skies:

"No place, there is no place
To hide the tongue of a fool.
The winds undo its grace
And spread it pole to pole,
Till every luck he had
Is squandered out in air,
And oh, but the birds are glad
For the secrets of that liar!"

## A Trim Reckoning

I could let Honor rot,
Thinking of one proud head
Strumpet Honor brought
To an incestuous bed,
Exacting as her fee
What honest whores despise,
The very mint of the heart
And coin of the eyes,
Till not a beggarwoman,
Borrowed child and all,
Had stew for her dinner,
Or pity for her soul—
Only a day gone hungry,
And Honor's lockers full.

## For a Going-Out

Because you will soon be gone,
And our busy hearts will lie
About the year's return,
And our busy fingers weave
A seemly dress for love,
Let us count peacefully
All we are masters of.

Elm, arcade, walk, and hall
Like laughter fall;
The iron cross goes down.
Eyes not our own,

Nor like our eyes, nor eyes,
Will mock up other skies
With signal passion.
And every man will fail
Whose passion is a pawn.

I live in this belief:
Archaic prayers prevail—
Faith in a cut stone,
Dancing for rainfall,
Goings-out, comings-in.
My loves, I cannot spell
Your passwords up or down,
Your songs in hell,
Your honor, or great pride,
Your name or changed face.
I can only tell
That once, in this place,
Apple-side, mountain-side,
Gray head and golden head,
One could call a man happy
Before he was dead,
In garden, steeple, desk,
Book, candle, or done task,
That made the seasons burn
In love's consuming name.

## GARDEN SET

1
It may be that the best, most blessed love
Is love of nothing. Rude japonica,
You shoot so from the roots, in bronze disguise.
I know you now, my beauty. Bring the shears!
Or all the lawns in Roanoke will die.
I keep the grass, my queen, to see you by.

2
Chrysanthemums, like words, grow tall too soon.
Down, Jumbo. Down, outrageous Miss Pompon.
Off with your head, Green Jack. Good warriors all,
Grow tough, grow double, practicing the fall.

3
I have a castle
Three stars high,

Tarragon and rosemary,
  Sang the garden child.

I have an apple tree
Two birds thick,
  Pokeweed, lopseed, daisy, dock.
  His eyes were mild.

Fetch me a coverlet
Four leaves thin,
  Lavender and cinnamon,
  To hide my song.

In a pasture wide as sleep
While the singing children make
  Music daylong.

4
Greystone William at your book,
Come look, come look!
When philosophy is spent
From the caterpillar's tent
Flies the bright moth of the air
Into nowhere.

5
Two ladies I remember from old songs:
This one that had a garden in her face,
Lily and rose she was, a summer place
Yearlong, a winter dream, lily and rose.

This other was a song or secret breath,
And where she sang, the maple came in leaf,
And where she went, myrtle and violet lay.
Her footstep made a summer. And which way
I care for, music-master, and which way
Is best, madrigal-maker, say, oh say!

6
Whether the gray sky over us
Listens, whitethroat, hears, chipping one—

Tchap, tchap, tuk, tuk, down dusk, up dawn,
All quick green spaces in between
Made gay—

There is not bird alone
Under the little leaves of the sun.

7
The gorgeous beetle loved Euphrosyne,
Evangeline loved he, douce Chatillon.
Three red and yellow graces in green weather
Called to the devil and the devil came.

8
For nothing at all but pleasure, rusty flag
And ragged purple flapper, do you wave?
A man could die in April, with the sky
In ribbons. Rabbi, only the grave would fail.

9
What more, what more, what more to love,
Light of August, distant dove?

I sing in the throat of a poet who is dead.
I sing because he is dead.
                      Make what you will
Of memory, Earth Mover, Master Mole.

Let the incredible phlox consume the hedge.
Let Madam Moon fill up the arms of night.

This dark, this light,
This past, this present—
Fie! It is enough.


## Suit

That time I was too proud,
Still decently arrayed,
To beg a coal or rag
Against my winter need.
But you, because you had known
Others come freezing back,
Thought to insure your own
Rich hearth from the weather's knock;
Flattered my strength, my sick
And unconditioned tongue,
And set me ears to win
Seasons beyond your home.

Do you think if you do not bind
My body in some cheap cloth,

That the gaudy stuff of the mind
Will keep me warm enough?
Think what a reed will cure
The desert eye of its tower
And palm-girt pool; what worn
Apple or bitter root
Restores a hungered throat
Better than heart-grown fruit.

I do not ask your treasure.
To refugees and the poor
A crust and a tin of water
Make grace at a rich door.
Let me add such a blessing
To begging love, no more.


## THE WINDS

The winds of space, spiced with the latest spring,
Even stinging on the lips like winter's strong
Unstoppered breath, are music. But my song
Stammers and breaks upon the winds of time.
My love, if you were only of this place,
Poor as perhaps it is, and death to face
Soon from the windy skies, still I could play
Notes that would turn black midnight to broad day,
Wounds to excuse for mercy, want to flood,
And pay all favors with my lung-driven blood.
But you go guarded from that tune, wrapped back
In some old concert of a summer night,
Or clash of bells against a freezing noon,
Deaf to the weather where I mark my time,
And time my enemy I cannot sing.


## TO WILLIAM WORDSWORTH
## FROM VERMONT

They laugh, bird-watcher, that you knew
Joy in rock, wood, river, or rainbow,
Or rather that the cliff moved, the night spoke,
The buck stood, and passion broke

The child's first heart. Not I.
I shed my hearts like sailors, growing by
Sunbreak or savor or seeds' press
Into the unsyllabled darkness
That raises all things bright,
Beautiful, fearful, moving, still:
The clouds contending, or the daffodil
That tossed the wandering sun a thousand ways
From English Ullswater.
In joy we start,
And grow by words apart.

On Glastenbury once I saw
The pale moon hesitate, but sky
And earth, divorcing, cast her free
Till cold on Pownal, cold on Bennington,
Her puppet light drained down,
And every eye she praised the valley long
Selected love.
Old puppet of the moon, this mountain night
More sharp with stars and waters than a dream
Of islands conjured in a poet's sight,
Not my eyes bless, but light.

And yet we half create,
As you say. The man has memory,
And quick as Adam's ear or Eve's bare eye
Was fruit and echoes, we are swords and fire,
Cities and song. We come trailing time
Like some old patchwork garment, half our own,
And, improvising fashions, stumble down
The path from chaos and old night. Undear
Things tutor us: not one pure voice
Across a field at evening, but a voice
Counties off, years off, crowds into that call
The sounds of an old summer, locusts in feather
Against a falling house, a ten-years-useless
Barn, the haunt of doves and secrets—all
The freight of sense, held easy, ready to spill
A lowland harvest on this granite hill.

       Old Rydal
Reaper of snows and fountains, every crop
Of every season's seedtime pushes up
Its blades to plume the pocked, perennial landscape.

Tintern, or ruinous
Tintagel, caves of Greece
And Cumae, cypresses
Winging the silver night at Arles, or meadows
Of childish May—low mint, lost irises—
Not light, but my eyes bless.


## THE SILO UNDER ANGEL'S GAP

The silo under Angel's Gap
Through garland orchards breaks in the morning light.
Forty times by the sun
My eyes have gathered June
And stored a heap of fodder in a bin.

Stalk over stalk, the green turned down to gold:
Whatever beat once on the bloody field,
Or split the roof of air.
Dido is there,
And the rag doll I murdered in the cold.

All mountains shrivel to some sort of food,
Eryx and Andes, Ida, Otter Peaks.
Mad David helps his eyes
To Adam's husbandries.
A tortured Jew translated by the Greeks

Leans out from heaven in pitiless mockery
Of the coarse bread and the raw dreggy wine,
Shadows that fire the gut
Until death puts them out
To feed the shadowy fish and Circe's swine.

I take these shadowy hills to fill my eye.
Shadow on shadow falls till it come night.
Helicon, Everest,
And Woody's barn at last
Ride with the moonless meadow out of sight

Into the fallow dark where blood and dreams
Refashion all the populace of day.
And forty bones that shook
When Eden's summer broke
Rehearse the garland rising in their clay.

## There Was a Bird

Love, I will tell you a tale.
There was a bird sang sweet,
A fabulous nightingale,
Had never a crumb to eat,
Never a bough to ride,
Only a voice, a voice,
That would strike the heart from your side
Out of all histories
Of any month but May,
Any scent but musk,
Till all you could taste was wine
In cool perpetual dusk.
Listening, you would smile
At heaven already heard,
Then you would ache a while
That you were not that bird,
No, nor that bird's mate
That you might fly with him
And sing at heaven's gate.
And your glad eyes would dim,
And you would taste your tears,
And feel the rise of the sun
Over the quartered years,
And feel your blood run on.

Tomorrow and today,
Every bird on his bough
Has more than heaven to say.
Love, shall I tell you how
Your face was bright, unkissed,
Your house the very land
Where hunger and danger vanished,
Or how your unclaimed hand
Held comfort? Shall I tell
I lost that foolish smile,
Remembered with a sigh
That paradise put by
As it were still to make
For pity, out of the thin
Rafters the winds shake,
Out of the winter moon,
Scant nourishment, full pain

Of labor, calloused skin,
And Graybeard looking in?

Shall I tell how I sing
To the beasts? Or how I pick
A feather for your cap
Out of the frosty patch,
A feather from the wing
Of the jay, maybe, whose blue
Blaze at winter's gate
Makes every bird more bright?

## Cirque d'Hiver

Could I have been a clown,
A raggedy tumbling man,
To paint my passions on,
Go little, or dress tall,
To tread a giant ball,
Or shed a burning suit,
To whistle a random note
Till all the children shout
At Jocko in the ring—

But no. I truly sing
Without the grace to call
The world and his heart a fool
Whose luck will always mend
For laughing on its end.
And all the children turn
Sick when the stilts burn
And the greasy colors run:
These tatters are my skin.

## A Ballad of Eve

The blessed worm of Eden sang
At my immortal ear:
The rose will riot on the vine
Year after year;

Night after night in love unbought
The man beside you lie,
And children run on painless feet
Around you day by day;

One god, of all the gods that be,
His table will suffice,
And hand and heart and tongue will know
No enemy but peace.

I walked alone into the dark,
Looking for my deed.
I struck my hand upon a rock
And could not make it bleed.

I lay across the lion's path
Who skirted softly on.
That whole wood was passionless
Up to the edge of dawn.

And there upon the bough it lay,
That made my first heart break.
With human hands I plucked the sky,
With human hunger ate.

And then such plenty was to do,
Danger and pride and pain,
It took me years to fashion true
God's dreaming song again,

The voice that doubled in my ear
Then, in my first of days,
And seasoned love with pity so
I had no tongue for praise,

That now sing back, daylong, the dark,
And nightlong sing the day
I walked the years from paradise
Where god beside me lay.


## THE SEASONS

1

Up, up, great blades. Grow green, you teeth of spring.
By Thebes it was, by Thebes I did my sowing.

The dragon made my apples. Wheat was born
Of his breathing face, and of his feathers, corn.
Shake out your leafy mane, America.
Grow great, Tehuantepec! Kenai, grow green!

2

It is not a maid and not a mother.
    Sing Persephone.
But yet a wife and yet a daughter
    Asleep under the tree.
May the twelve winds of the sky
Move together quietly,
And the quarreling waters run
So smooth the blackest sands are warm
At the water lily's root.
Stop the melon, hold the fruit,
Hear the sleeper's heart in dream
Breathe like children: Proserpine.
    Child and queen, Proserpina,
    Light and softest love, stay near.

3

Run, Master Merlin, Camelot is down.
Gorgon is dead. A city that was not stone
Rose on a harp, a harp of holy air.
Arthur, alas! Alas, proud Guinevere,
And all the pretty swords that kept the hall!
A rubble of proud names, a stony tale.

4

Taliesin, Taliesin,
Years upon the sea he lay.
Taliesin, Taliesin,
First a man and then a boy,
Sang the letters of the wood,
How the oak and ash were laid
In leafy battle side by side,
Told us how the world began,
First a boy, then a man,
Years he lay beneath the snow.
Taliesin, raise us now.

# A Journey

You are always walking away
With the light, bright journeyman.
I wander under the leaves
Of the old town.
The signal hours fall;
Shop, office, hall
Attend, as if the sun
Could never say farewell.
I must make the sun my own.

For the traveller travels well,
Carrying songs to spend,
Branches whose touch can heal,
Seed for new land.
Yet travels heavier
Returning, from the freight
Of foreign syllables,
Beasts crying at night,
Pulses of wind, and hot
Odors that grow
Nerves in the traveller
Where no nerves were.

Now in Virginia
The orange lilies patch
June's raggedy green dress.
Some apples have red rust.
It has all happened before.
What should we be but poor?

The hours answer.
In the central dark
Where we are not loved enough,
Something heavy as gold
Glints by the mineshaft:
The sun in a vein of rock,
Beating mysteriously!
Children at nightwork
Lament the murdered day,
Tremble at what is not
Departure, but a way
Of rising up to walk
When the rock rolls away.

## For Christmas, 1960

I think, this winter night,
Child of a crooked house,
Of every path made straight
Across a wilderness.

To Carthage many a one,
Cathay and Darien—
And Palinurus drowned,
And Dido left to mourn,

And Egypt's horse beneath
The crude returning seas,
And Montezuma ruined:
All flights, all entrances.

The scorn of Pharaoh drove;
The acrid cloud on Troy;
Guinevere's, Helen's gold;
Allspice and ivory,

To bones in the Southern Cross,
Cripplings of fire and ice,
Fruited Americas,
And Everest at last.

Old leaves, this winter night,
Shift at the locust's foot,
Random as the hope
Our newest pilgrims take

For city, song, and kin,
For beauty, pride, and lust.
Be with us in the air,
Old sibyl voices. Dust

Can ride the winds of space
To find the mouth of hell,
Birdless as ever, close
As Cumae in the soul;

Or near as Bethlehem,
Across the years of light,
Some harbor for the son
Of man, companioned bright

By stars that never were:
Columbus' lode, or pure
Galahad's spy that drove,
Clear as consuming love,
Through semblance, season, scar,
To manger and to shore.

From *Adam's Dream* (1969)

## Tallis' Canon

The dawn wind smelling of smoke
from the smouldering trash gulley breathes me awake.
I can imagine the lake
rippling its dark taut silk a moment, and the breeze
like a cloud-shadow moving to pick up
its invisible particles of smoke.

Dawn-wind, pick up
my prayer coming awake
from the dangerous dark
bloodside of the world,
and soon with the sun
in the still unseen regular dawn
forgotten:

to feel the day
flow into my limbs, coming back
from sleep, or going away into love.

Lord, that I am a moment of
your turnings.


## 1  Diurne

All day on my hill the sun turns over,
the blackbird lifts his bill from the water,
the brown bird dozes in the vine,
the slow cows wander
for shade; petal and blade
deepen and shine, spray out and gather.
In his secret weather under the urn
the slug all flesh lifts up a delicate horn.
All day the quail cries falling
into the corn, and the corn greening.

Only my man,
lacking his body's language, calls a name.

## 2   NOCTURNE

In the night called morning, the body turning
with seas held steady in their beds
washes, like them, and tides,
quicksilver running, shattered and gathered, moon and stars
cooling and warming; breathes, is breathed
by airs not animal, by planets burning
down years of light.

Sleep, wake, sings the body, never lonely,
nameless as leaves in their riding, falling,
moving as saps and stems move, crying
as birds cry, never dying.


## BLUE

Bird, I name you, from your feather, blue,
and blue from cornflower, flower from sky,
and sky from water, as if all blue things
were blue together. Thus did Adam make
a world of blue, that rose on the bird's back
to the cloud, and from the cloud cried, God!
And Adam trembled, for the sky was red,
the bird was yellow, and the field was green,
and he was still alone.


## TWO-PART SONG

Between the gourd and the worm
poor Jonah sang
to black leviathan,
"Bury me, bury me,
beast, at the tempest's foot,
and rock me down
under the hunting wind,
under the suing sea;
breathe me, unmuscle me;
come, be kind."

Between the worm and the tree
poor Jonah saw

the shadow of a hand.
The hand sang, "Jonah,
Jonah, why so hot
for sorrow? Did the brute
heed your command?
Will the undoing sun?
Do you spit cities down?
Come, Jonah. Stand."


## CHARITY BEGINS . . .

The farm boys, forbidden my company
(I own cards and whiskey), cry
down the cowbarn hill in the baptist day
at the hot games of children on holiday.

Come, my brother, my keeper the farmer, come,
let us reason together in the old tongue
of the cricket and worm as they sing
to each other under the warm
boy-high hay: from Hell's harm
and all manner of corruption defend us. Make the corn
sweet and scatter the birds of prey.
May they crash on the rocks and wash in the marshes, while we
perform our singular duty.
     Oh John
Hardison, John Hardison, how easily you
hate! Are you sure you have got
Jesus every day of the week? I haven't.
I could curse my forward hands that found
cookies the quickest way to the mind
of your dirty children, and raised the rage
of Heaven on their innocent cheating heads
when I suggested the movies.
And on mine, in mine, where the incomplete tongue dwells
to meet your kills
of the woodchuck under the hedge, and the stray cat,
and the fledgling sparrows easy to hit.
In your bottom, every stranger
is a trespasser. So be it.

So bless you that I know
how hugely our hurt hearts grow, by their wounds,

for the hymn-singers, and for the sake
of the hymned who alone can take
into his warfaring dark heart
the chick and the stoat, and make light
of all sinners.


## The Bennett Springs Road

I knew it was there, if I'd had time to look:
the sweet water falling over rock,
the leaf-mold floor, secret to all but light,
the tall boles stationed between day and night.

This is the heart of the mountain, not the crest.
Season and century league in some high place,
impulsive powers that beat the peak to sand
and scatter Appalachian on the wind.

And lie at last by the little stream that brings
all gods to truth. On the road to Bennett Springs,
tired of the paltry ridges, I lay down
the last of my youth where all the gods had grown,
became the water falling over the stone,
became the forest-father to red men,
became the tribe of stars, both daughter and son,
the mother of moss, the bird that sang I am.


## Starlings

Awkward and natural
as children's drawings,
these squabblers, even among themselves, for fat-
back and peanut butter—they can make
(bob-tail, flat-foot, gold only at the beak)
a whole tree speak.

And if they—
motes in the sun's eye, rough
grains in the wind's breath—alight
on grass, all flesh, close up:
look! look!
More shimmering than snow

iced over, oh
more rich, for being real, than night,
their dark
heart-feathering, rare-recovering, leaping-up
and raven rainbow!


## THE FASCINATING WORLD OF FUNGI

> Despite popular belief to the contrary, there is only one practical way of distinguishing between edible and poisonous toadstools, but the result may not profit a man.
> —John Ramsbottom, Keeper of Botany, British Museum

A fairyland indeed, the whole wood sprung
overnight, it seems, in yellow, white, and brown,
in red, in tawny olive, pink, and fawn.
And not smooth only: scaly, spotted. One
with a cat's-paw track, one warted, one with a stem
like locust, deeply rutted; one a blade,
the "Beef-Steak Fungus," *Langue de Boeuf;* a sponge,
Sparassis; and a cornucopia,
Craterellus, Horn of Plenty.

The impeccable tongue
of John Ramsbottom, Keeper: "The eating
of large quantities, particularly unaccompanied
by other food, is likely to cause
wishful reflection."
Amanita: Death Cap—a serum
has been developed, but another treatment
consists "in feeding a patient
the whole stomachs of three rabbits, chopped up with the brains
of seven. . . . It has been said,
in favor of the treatment, that seven rabbits
are more readily procurable
than serum, and that these
need not even be lost to the table."
I should have thought
Dr. Stevens more readily procurable
than seven rabbits, albeit a loss to the table.

But why rout
Dr. Stevens from Troutville, if the experience
of one's predecessors counts?

"Strange and new fangled meates"?
But well known to the Ancients.
"To nature and dygestion
peryllous and dredfull," by a late *Great Herball.*

All innocent
the wood's floor blossoms.
The Keeper impeccably reasons:
"Indiscriminate eating . . . may render the consumer meet
for repentance
or beyond it."


## The Writer Indulges a Hobby

We searched the wood again
for mushrooms, after the last rain. In a mile or so
found only a few. Then, coming back,
saw dozens sprung beside our very track,
like leaves, like nuts, like chips of shale,
pale as a sunpatch, dark
as a waterstain, and all before unseen.

To the eye grown quiet on its spot,
fields open out their greens,
and every green his shape,
and every shape his shadow moving slow,
a nothing, a steeple-head in the sun's eye,
an ant on the steeple-bush, and in his jaw
a grain, and in that grain a cell . . .
It is only to tell
over again, how much we overpass,
walkers on dust, walkers on grass.

To tell the salamander from the leaf,
look out the stages of the Emperor's life,
to hear the vireo where we have sought her
is like walking on water.


## On Not Getting the Phono Fixed

It has been on the list for a week, along with "laundry,"
and "check with Shirley," and "pick

up cartons for apples." Twice it says
"take vic."

But I haven't, though two new discs have come
from the Heritage people, and Frank has returned
my Civil War Songs that were gone
all summer, probably warping on his floor.

It is like fasting, that discovers
the body to itself, the space between skins, the power
in soft sacs, the secretions of
sublingual glands, and the enormous will
in empty hands.

Or exploring a steep hill
with rocks, where there are supposed to be snakes
and even wildcats
in the caves,
but no water, and nothing to eat,
so that spending the night
is about as near to death as you can get
in this country, given the earth
without man,
the land without invention,
unless you count
Monkshood, or Mountain St. Johnswort.


## MAIL

The letters come and go,
saying Stay so,
saying Don't mention that
ever again, saying Please speak,
but do not go so deep,
saying Am in great pain,
Am having a wonderful time,
Remember, Grow, Stand up,
Buy me, but am not cheap,
saying Spare me, Work,
Only believe, Lie low.

In the letters, the seasons come and go.
It is fall in Cincinnati. It is summer in Mexico.
Mother is at the Plaza next week.

Martha has broken her ankle.
Billy is well, thank you.
When are you coming to Chapel Hill?

Isn't the best time spring? If I can get
ahead of the work. I have a book
you will like. I have a Camembert, K.589
(though not a fine recording), the catalog
with the King Alfreds and the Red Marleys, and the thing
to dig the holes with.

But which one of me shall I bring?


## INSOMNIA

See here, children, it's time to sleep.
Alice, pull in your long neck.
Sylvia, sheathe your teeth. And lie down, Maggie,
there's a good girl. And Emily,
turn off the hose, and George,
for godssake don't snore. Dear Charlotte, ghosts
do not visit our shore, you're only pretending.
Miriam, stop beating
that drum, and Joan,
one cannot sleep in a crown.

There, there, Mother will tuck you in. Cleo will prowl the hall
a while, but she's old enough
to make her own decisions. Before you start to drink,
practice at home. Be glad
you had tolerant parents. Ruth, you pray too much.
Virginia, did you wind the watch? No, Jeep,
it's not a man, it's a possum.

        Oh my own,
will you go to sleep now? will you leave me alone?


## LEGEND

The lady lily-farmer
broke me a tremendous head,
six pale tongues curling under,
spotted and streaked with blood.

She said it would keep in water
for weeks, and it did.

That was the summer the dog died,
a drought year.
The small crops paled in the air;
the blacksnake fled to the bottom; a great fire
seared three sides of the mountain. In my room
the heavy scent of the flower crept and clung
like a live smoke. Far in the north
my father sickened. When I tried to make love,
I wept.

You can say there was no connection.
The gardener was dark and tiny. For her work
she wore men's jeans, and a man's battered hat
that she pushed back when she spoke. She was leaving that town
for farther south.

My talisman,
if that is what you make it, never grew
in Mrs. Garrett's garden.
When I threw it out,
the rains came. All of this is true.
The farmers would have got on anyway, the old men died
anyway, my bones have stiffened in their pride.
But say this to the Virginians: I have had a god
in the house. Say I have weathered my death
again. Say Triton. Or say Proteus.


## Loving 1

I went a journey round the world of my body,
hitherto unexplored except in theory
conned in the class of Professor Ptolemy.

He mapped me well, knew where my sun was,
told me which routes to take, like Rand McNally
told me how to get to Indianapolis,
but couldn't describe the look of the place.

So I knew you were there. And I spelunked in the caves
and slippery passages, often on my knees,
tapping with my bonestaff, or climbing,
sometimes, on gray wires,

or lanterning, or calling, till I reached my skin
and sweated across it. But the sun
was farther, farther, forever not to be had.
It was then, I think, I called the cartographers bad.

Do not take the inland route, is my advice.
There are incomparable views of ice,
and jungle ambuscades still to be feared
on the southern roads, where the natives have not been cleared
out. I would say: Sail, sail
beyond the Islands of Spice, with the sun west,
the sun always other, the sun in an outer space.
How can we map what moves us? How can we tell
the risks of scouting?
If we fail, we fail.


## Loving 2

I tried to find you in the tongues of my body,
along the walls of my heart,
baled in the cords of my eyes, or bound
in my brain's knot.

I knew you were there, you must have been, from my sap
gone tropic, bending after the leave of the light
that was in me, in me, growing me up to be
myself entire in my completed body.

Then I tried how my tongue would speak you, or how my hand
would feed you, how my blood would clear and run
with your color. What I heard
was my praise and pleasure drumming from my own skin
by my own bonesword.

Oh is loving leaning all the ears of the body
to the winds, and what they sing?
holding the cells' breath in bright study?
listening? listening?


## As Theory

If they should come to praise me
when I no longer want

and ask me how I fashioned
a thing so elegant,
who seem a simple woman
that all the tradesmen know,
shall I adjust my hat, and touch
my hair, and shall I say
(being too old for mockery),
"I did it for a man
who would not hear a wonder
in the old common tongue,
and so I made a shape of it
to suit his fancy eye,
intricate as the emperor's bird,
mechanic, like a toy"?
They will not understand me,
but you, if you should hear,
could teach it to the tradesman's boy
as theory, my dear.


## Pietà: December

The valley in the hills' arms. Mist.
All things sad-colored as a stone.
I cannot tell which outline is my own,
field, flesh, or choking weather,
dun beast at byre, the wilted snows,
your image in my tears,
fathered apart, but grown my second sight.
Beast, body, babe? Pressure of hand and voice,
gait, shoulder, foreignest and nearest face.
No woman is blessed. Though winged all ways
new Aprils summit, Mary keeps old eyes
for failure, for each brother of her blood
broken.

Old hills, cradle her sapling, her waste weed,
each in his own dimension. God
did not deceive her sorrowing, for whom
the tomb will never empty of its earth
though every sun in heaven break forth.

## Letter

The heat is terrific. The storms are terrible.
I have revised the tool closet. They are coming along
on the Science Building. They do not light
the altar at night. They have littered the lawn
with prunings from the elm.

It will not change here.
The mountains are one face.
A peasant said she'd watched the mountains grow
for thirty years. I know that is not true,
even without the texts. It is slow, slow,
earth's crust, rising and falling. The lavender
wild bergamot is in bloom, and the big-root
morning-glory that furls up at night.
I have watched it, like I watched the cereus,
once, in an elegant parlor, bloom in an hour.
You cannot see them move, but they must.
It is like breathing. It is made clear in the text:
ripening, rottening. The proprietor
of the elegant parlor, a sixty-year-old widower,
made lead soldiers for a hobby, especially
historic grenadiers, dragoons, and lancers.

I have cut my hair again. I have put up
the family photographs. Mother said
no one would know who that girl—herself—was.

Have you found a new face
in your foreign desert?
Is space a constant mirror, and is time
its constant image, or vice versa?
You left the light on in the basement.
Your empty parking-slot and unkempt yard
image you like a mold. I can fill them in
with the old features. I do not feel love loosening.
Do forms harden in time?
It is not made clear in the text.
Do mountains grow?
Sometimes I think we are all illiterate,
breathing like lilies; spread so, furl so.

## Histoire

All night the owls like death hung over
the sanctuary wood. I thought
of the furred throat, of the flowers
furled in shame. Worse, of the red men
haunting like owls the settlements.
Too close, too close. And I in my pine bed
stiffened, felt the feathered head
hover, the eyes
strike, the uplifted stone
sever. All slow, like years.
When the scream came,
the day-bird's and my own as one,
I hid this dream away from love and lover.


## Santa Maria delle Grazie

The wall that's faded like some rich old rug
brought from the East—how many hearts
have walked here, light and heavy, or eyes rubbed
the nap away, trying to see God
in a familiar dress, blue over red,
speaking and breaking bread?

Oh, rub it all away, and let him be
nothing but memory:
a song or family saying saved from childhood,
the copper shine in some lost household;
else the expectancy already fled
forward from faces of the newly dead.


## Adam's Dream

1
Once a deep sleep
Adam slept,
lily and rose
to light his dream,
bird and beast to keep him warm,
and stars to sing.

When Adam woke,
when Adam woke,
all the silver waters broke,
all the beasts stood up to mourn,
and the maple and the thorn
laid down their leaves
when time began.

Silver cities rise and fall
for Adam's dream.
Mountains crumble, planets cool
for Adam's dream.
Adam's neighbor, Adam's son
watch the sea swing up and down,
roast and shiver, spit and turn
for Adam's dream.

The ribs of love,
whose bones are they?
Star of winter, rose of May.
Did I dream
so fair a thing
between my sleep
and my waking?

2
Between my sleep and my waking
lives all fashion of forsaking.
Every feather, every crust,
every rafter dust, dust.

Between my waking and my sleep,
birds fly, roots creep.
Greenleaf come on Adam's tree
once I saw, or thought I saw.

3
Once I lay
where Adam stood.
Day's eye, night's lid.
And dreamed a dream out of my side
and woke and it was blood.

Once I stood
where Adam lay.
Night's lid, day's eye.

Stood up in my blood and wept
over Adam where he slept.

4
Shall I press the oak
for my increase?
Shall I press the perishing sun
for peace?

What shall abide
the wind and the rain?
Shall Adam's garden
come again?

Shall Adam's angel
welcome me,
or only the wind
in the time-tree?

5
Manshape, mudfoot,
windy tongue, snowheart.

What sea
cast up
hawk wing,
acorn cup?

What star
sang down
kin cry,
kingdom?

Manshape, lightfoot,
ghost-tongue, fireheart.

6
Between two dreams,
bloody and rare,
my heartways cross.
A shade hangs there.

When I awake
I am a man.
The waters carry
what time began.
The waters carry
what time did not:

river-rider, wordweight,
heart's light, manshape.

7
When the nerve of day is struck,
Adam, what shall be my light?
Who shall take it from my side?
Will it breathe? And will it bleed?

Shall I know it for my mate?
Shall I fear it? Shall I get
breed that couples in the dark?

Angel, Angel, Adam's guest,
count the cages of my breast,
cut my bones as clean as light,
if I wake, or if I sleep.

8
At the root of Adam's tree,
woundmaster, grow me.
Ditchdrought, hailstone,
blood rot, stranglevine.

Strike down the arrow of your peace.
Pierce wintergloom, heart's ease.
Press sycamore, press star of night.
Oak's sap, heart's height.
All men one bone,
Lord of clay and heaven, one,
Adam's dream under the sun.


## Singing Christmas

We are in love with beginnings, and the power of beginning
in all things: seeds, the voice breaking into song,
cubs, the steel ribs of the Science Building.
     *King Jesus hath a garden.*

However humble: the bird-beak cutting its shell;
however painful: I will turn from this house, and go;
miraculous: chromosomes drilling, the uncanny split in the cell.
     *Matris in gremio.*

We sing, we sing, our faces bright with mourning,
at the funeral door that even grass can enter,
for the split seed in the field born over and over.
                      *In the bleak midwinter.*

Not for a name, for shepherd, king, or cradle;
not for a time, when time is turned again
out of his grave by brute and bearing April.
                      *How far is it to Bethlehem?*

But for all times when driven night turns over
a new shoot to the sun, and sparrows greet us
in a new tongue, and kiss their bread and water.
                      *Qui nobis est natus.*

And for all spaces opening: the sky,
the wave, the crust of pent Antarctica,
the heart hoarding its blood, the winter eye.
                      *Alleluya.*


## Xmas Shopping

At Christmas now imported yew
and holly weave the natural year
around the phone poles. In the streets
of Baltimore, O Say, I hear
electric voices in the air
proclaim some world of kings and sheep,
but all the proper suburbs stare
with ruddy eyes at worlds they know.
Mrs. Pulinski lost her fare
at Woolworth's in the plastic snow
and had to walk to Dundalk.

                      Now
Towson's giant tree unpins the sky
of planets for her golden boughs.
Miraculous, the spent star glows
above the Plaza. In true green
the needles of the Christmas pine
at York and Chesapeake humbly wait
the ride to Hampton, the odd freight
of cane and candle—twelve dry days
to sanctify the children's mess,
then out upon the guilty heap

of leaves and prunings, tinseled yet
in ragged streamers for the nest
of summer's mocking breast.

Beneath their vague commercial cheer,
Northwood and Park Heights Avenue
unite more deeply at New Year
than, drinking separately, they know
to hail the common mystery
once proudly hailed: Persephone
gone underground, but peasant love
left living by the barter of
the blood of innocents; the flight
to Egypt, the returning light
that grew, and Lazarus lived by it,
and Simon cast and filled his net.

God's seed, the seasonal tree, the blood
sliding from pole to slippery pole,
dip down, like banners bravely hung,
to frosty execution.
The rocket's glare meant life, that now
leaves bloody entrails on the snow
for picking soothsayers; my tongue
means love, but says destruction.

When shall great-bodied August grow?
What sleeps in starcast darkness now?
What savage histories await
the calendars of blood and state?
Indifferent to metaphor,
the neon and the native fir
reply in points of hope and fear:
Time is not lasting—season, night,
invention, marvel, human shape,
the city's map. Old Bethlehem's street
at Easter wound to Olivet,
but shone, like Hutzler's ritual light,
in dark December, briefly bright.

## Sans Day Carol

On Eden the snow fell
in winter, winter.

What shall be coal
to my fire?

Who is my brother
all the white weather?
Where is his footprint
over the sea?

River by river
stony I wander.
Blade in the water
and spear in the sky

scissor my winter
wider than blood!
Bear me as tidings,
rose and redbird,

runnel and living star
over my head.
   *And Mary bore Jesu*
   *that rose from the dead.*


## Derivative

When I compose "the alphabet of bone,"
I hear you, Emily Dickinson,
a long way from the schoolroom, in the back garden,
perhaps, over the marjoram and dill,
planning the evening meal.
The family's out, but you are not alone.

I am learning, too, the kinship of the bee,
the types of sparrow, every pulsation of weather,
how beasts are born, how quinces burden the tree;
how, as the honey's made, our poetry
makes out our given nature,
and how the separate feature
dissolves in the accomplished critic's eye.

I have tried to grow,
forty drought summers, flowers from the seed.
I have hoed, trenched, and weeded. I have discovered
the dahlia's laws; that cutting back
makes vinca shoot all over; that mint root

is uncontrollable. I might have read this
in a garden book, but would not have believed it.

Would hardly believe, still, in anything perennial,
the hardy word fallen on fresh soil,
a season's color but a husband's luck
in cultivation.

Yet I've seen you send a poem you've cut
like pansies from the stock
the careful Pilgrims brought—so here's my packet
to press in the memory-book. I know a few things by heart:
carpel from corn, how crocus grow, how blue is shut
in the jay's egg, how my separate songs
are yours also.


## Farmer Blake

1
A spade of speech invented whole
from my limbs' wood and loins' oil,
that would I have for my life's tool.

And turn with it, and turn with it
a terrain yet unmined of man,
not some cisalpine Rubicon,
Achaean cave, or Syrian desert.

Be this my green and pleasant land,
the common field of tares and corn,
where I would plant myself and sing
how man is born, how man is born.

2
I dug a garden deeper down
than roseroot or dividing worm,
past buried babes I once had known
and past their father's published name,

until, when spade could strike no stuff,
but swung on void bottomless,
I cursed me for a laboring fool
and flung off my depending tool

and followed him into the wound
and struck the earth on which I stand,

brother to birds and the north wind
whose roots are not in any ground.

3
I farm the air with my bright tongue.
A farmer was my father's name,
who left me flints and blades of stone
and acres where no blood had been.

This is the land, he said. Grow it,
brief as lily, deaf as chuck.
Servant to stars and coming light
is my bloodroot, he said. Grow it.


## A Meditation in Time of War

The Curriculum Committee
is meeting in the Board Room of the Library
deciding whether a familiarity
with Xenophon is essential
to the educated man.

Downstairs in periodicals
the dirty newsprint tells
in half a dozen languages (but all
Greek) how blood still reaches the sea
out of Asia,
Africa, Chicago,
out of the Library window
where the Judas tree
blazes one root,
road rather, out of the heart
of every humanity.

All we can betray
is the facts.

I usually put
History on the kitchen floor, against dog tracks,
boot tracks, sink splashes, and spilled beer.
The tortured children stare
up, and remind me of the dead
no-name of suffering unsuffered
massy creation. I have had
my world as in my time: beer in the hotel bed-

room, publication, and promotion.
I have had property, and found it good,
oiling the kneehole desk, and the upright knees.
I have dressed for faculty teas.
I have taught how the poet felt
in Cumberland, the hills about his head,
flat France a memory, and the unwed
partner of his child
paid off. "The weather was mild
on Sunday, so we walked to Gowbarrow." I walked to Carvin's Cove
with the dogs. My cousin Xenophon
broke camp, and marched
out of the parched basin
toward the redeeming sea that smacked of home.
The tide for Athens! and the long watch
toward the prophet slain,
and exile over again.

The sun wings downward toward the time to drink.
The sea is very far, and yet I hear
untidy sailors in the stacks
weary from ropes, and swearing. And I think
of Grissom walking weightless into the sun.
And yes, I think
I will vote for Xenophon.

# 1 Jan 66

We know. We have heard the news in the dark of our ears.
We have changed the calendars. We are resolved
to abide by the calendars, resolved
it is not our will that turns the year, but ours
to owe him our small powers, hoping to be
by his regular grace, sun-lucky; hoping to flower,
make glad the eye, make apples for the poor,
or failing election, make compost and straight timber.
We know it will be all right, if we do not assert
that we know anything, or want anything, saving only
our peace. That love on these terms will come.
But alone in the room
of war and winter, the child barely born
cries out, I am cold, I am hungry, I want light.

We know, we say, and do away with the dark
and the news and the calendars, too small to wait.

## Falling Dead

A swallow caught in the old chimney
beat all day, a heart of the house, consigned
to slow exhaustion or a hard stun.
No one could concentrate. Even the flies
shunned the old flue. It was only the noise,
but I thought, with the common flourish: they know, they must know.

When I tried the tin block, it gave with a fall of rubble and soot.
Two dips about the parlor, and the bird
exited to the chicory and rain.
It happens over and over again.

In the country, things fall down.
The Humane Society does not come.
Bulldozer, nettle, vine—
Last year Jean's mare
writhed so all night on her side, she left
twelve square feet of bald pasture. You clear
them off your land, or you leave them there,
woodchuck, shoat, hare.
You are not squeamish. You know you will never know
your own end. But look, snake-friend;
see, skunk-litter; here, another swallow.
I think of you in the air, in the ivy-root, or quick in cool water.
My fields stand dear
from your falling. Summer by winter
I glean from you, friend craven mouse,
the secrets of my house,
maybe my calling.

## Hello, Betsy Parrish

Hair swinging, dressed for riding, a student lopes
across the patch.
A hail springs to my lips,
"Hello, Betsy Parrish."

The dog barks,
but she does not stop.

She is not Betsy Parrish, who once went,
hair swinging, dressed for potting, maybe dancing,
across another lot
under another mountain, another sun
on a day now twenty years done.

Now twenty years the same sun
rising, the same voice falling on the air.
Elizabeth has a family in Des Moines,
probably; is one of the pillars
of the League of Women Voters.
I have not been anywhere.

Loved the same man with three faces,
kept my original parents, gone to stare
at the daylight-saving leaves in the same places
at the same times, all in the one year,
and kept up Bach at recess *(Gottes Zeit
ist die allerbeste Zeit)*, after Mozart.

We do not choose. Time does not touch our faces.
Only the tongue of greeting leaps or lags.
Only the ears are deaf. Hello, Betsy Parrish
over the patch, in muddy riding togs.


## Sabbatical

In general I dislike cleaning house, taking stock,
rearranging the office. It's nice when it's done,
but doing it takes such a long time. This year I finally collected
three boxes for the Goodwill, plus some worn-out suitcases.
But they wouldn't call, so I
got in touch with the Salvation Army. Now there's space
to breathe in. I am forty-three.
Years haven't heaped anything on me.
I even sold the Steinway. What was the point,
with three keys gone, and one finger-joint
stiff as a rail? I don't think
it was failure or laziness always to repeat
the same sonata, always to stare at the same mess
in the closet. The dust has a business

which the dust doesn't know. I will never (the dust tells me)
play the piano. I will never write
the article on Tennyson. I will never have children. I will never go
to Greece. I will never see
my mother again, or Brownie.

On the other hand, I have finally gotten some peace.
A cleared house looks like a lessening. But the clothes
we kept hanging around, thought we might wear sometime,
or the ones we've outgrown—everybody knows getting rid of them
is no such thing. Now I concentrate
the party dress on the left, the school on the right,
and jeans I don't bother to put away: one set on the chair,
one set in the laundry. And where
I used to stack up books from the library,
I keep a flower or two: rosemary
for remembrance, goat's rue—

And soar into clean air
like a transplant or new shoot
from the mother-root, or like a bush grown thick
from cutting back. But my bloom
will fail me, and I dread
another start-of-term. Not all my dead
approve me. I've mislaid
my Modern Novel notes, and I'm afraid
the Valley Cleaners lost my winter coat.
I mustn't forget to bring the dahlia-root
inside. This year the golden ones look good.


## Staying at Home

Travellers, I've your journeys here before me:
Seine-side and Tiber-side the civil quays
gray in the dusk, and the stone exaltations
waver and die. The fishers will soon put out
from Atrani, and their simple lamps like stars
show the high watcher where Aeneas' oars
dripped with the vanished waters, under spars
travelling from Ida . . .

Journeying
fills up the heart so, rooms and rooms. I've thought
how this one brings an armory, and that one

a chapel lit for prayer. Or here comes home
an antelope stained dancing into stone.
Why, then,
not open house, and entertain the eye
with spoils of Lachish, aisles of Salisbury,
or from the plain
those monoliths reared temple-wise again?

What eye can carry, or what heart can place,
or ear enjoin to music—if there's one
hall to contain, we love its spaciousness.
And who walks there is Master. But shall I
serve graven history?
When Francis cast his seed, it was his tree
sent down the shade; when Joan lit France,
it was his fire; and where the whore
of Baghdad flexed, it was his floor.

My narrow house
suffices me for space, if here
the leaves are lived in, and each year
turns down its secret of becomingness
to cold December. Here's a color,
bright lily or dun sparrow,
for his gallery; I offer
my song to his ear; I spring my young
for his interpreting; my crop
to plume his land; my red
roof for his sheltering; my dead
to warm his hand.


## End of Leave

The day the cow stepped on the bicycle
was the day: summer is over. No more biology,
but only history, history, history.
                                      No more
wind in the hair, for the hair must be set,
and the windshield wiped against the wet
ruin of sight.

For I cannot see
(says history) through a bead of rain. I cannot hear

with too much wind in my ear, and too much green
defaces my fair city.

To live as a green thing
is to live alone. Human action
requires a gray suit, a raincoat,
a comb, a contraceptive, and a hat.

Put away
your poplar-skin; put in
your glass eye; fear stone.


## GROUND GLASS

One morning, set
among leaves by the maple-root, some jet
fragment, some blue or paste
glinter without a clue
awakes in my clay
(or the sparrows'). Yesterday
I raked seed-hulls away
from that spot. Nothing was there
but drought-bare
August under the feeder.

Yet it is hard to pry loose this rider
of groundswells, cast sharp
to my hand, hard to round
bowl, canister, or family circle.

So poems rise to the mind as curious
shards of some shop or house. And was I there
familiar? of use? and was I bought
or fused perhaps on the spot? And did I stand
sound for a while, before I fell to ground?


## EARTH SCIENCE

1
Perhaps, in arid lands, by that dead sea,
the blood is larger, does not beat
so with the lilac, turn so with the worm
on the pavement after a summer storm?

Yet I read of an English lady
who made a garden with the local flowers
outside Jerusalem, so it looked like home.

2

I believe in a native father, perhaps with red hair,
and a mother who, in the common way,
took in the kiss, bore out the curse of power.

I believe in the blood
turning small, as it must, in the evening hour,
turning down with the sparrow,
convicted by the vein in the cut hay.

That morning's artery beats up
I thank their sensual sap
who were not in the beginning,
are now, are not.

3

Under his hands
the corners of the sky unfolded lands.
The kingdoms
of hills and fishes praise him.
How, then, single a man?

By his forked tongue
about the garden:
my flesh, my bone,
my house, my lot,
my sun and moon,
my fire and heat,
my showers and dews,
my nights and days,
my frosts and snows,
my praise.

4

That tradesman called his son—
flowers spread for him, and birds flew down;
blind heads, like evening stars, grew bright;
fish multiplied; sore beggars sheltered
under his hem; his tongue
found out the worm's words; his vein
ran with the lamb's blood; he reproved
the owning eyes of women, and the stone
of righteousness that sang, " I judge."

"I love," he said, "the cool of the hedge
where sparrows come, at evening."

5

Under a garden wall, by night,
a prayer's space, he felt his blood go great.

Hands over him, like light,
folded the corners of his grief
small as a falling leaf.

6

Peter, my brother, the olive, the cock
(he sang) crow up,
and Caesar pace his court.

Angels, living and dead,
ringed round his head.

He hung
in the oak's pain.
He sang:
praise heaven.

He sang: go small as the ribbon
in the cell. King David's thigh
is gone a harp-string and a bone.

He sang: the blind shall see
by my body on his winds
brushing the ends of the earth together.
My words, he sang, will coin that weather
where you will see
the English lady,
your mother, your red father.

7

I sing, I sing
breadcrumb and broken blood.
I see, I see
my ash-tree, my children, my servant-maid,
my house, my bird-wing,

shalestone, sunset,
great Caesar's stewardship.

And may I slip
the stones of his gate

with the small cells of grass
till everlastingness.


## THE RING

I will try to be exact.
I was lying down last night with my eyes shut,
but this was not a dream. I was awake in my room.
A dog turned; the truck tires sounded
like an intense wind off the Interstate.
Then they were silent.

I cannot say by what light I saw it,
both saw it and was in it, like all our sight
and all we claim to create:
something of me is in this word, and yet
the word is separate.

My body, lying down, was surrounded
by what I will call a ring, but without extent.
It was not made of any element
that we know, not light, not air,
not water; but earthiness was entirely absent
from it. I will call it power,
for it lived, but not with our atomic life.
It had presence, but no shape. It did not speak.
To say so would be a projection of our categories
(and I have heard, in other circumstance, that other voice
with my skin ear, my echo ear, that needed then
to be Job's child, commanded to rejoice
when all excuse for love was lost).

No. It was as if the spirit breathed,
without a lung, its peace; or the forked tongue
followed its other way, not that of speech,
but gesture. There is language in a stone,
as every poet knows; as every lover
spells, in his ecstasy, illiterate bone.

It promised nothing, not being made of words
or of blood, that can invent. It did not imply
our only heart's desire: you have been sent.

It was power, power that stood by
for all our needs, and seemed to say
(for I must phrase it): here am I. Take me.

I have done nothing all day but stare
at the dishes, and read Wordsworth
on hiding-places, him who knew so well
what we see clear, but clumsily half-tell.

I walked by the stream. The hay was loud
with bugs escaping; they know
what danger is. I too
feared once the many-bladed mower.
Once, but not now.


## The Wall

I stand on both sides of the wall. Myself in the sun
calls to myself in the dark, who is asleep,
possibly dead. Inside the dream
the wall is gray, a grave edge
seen from beneath. Bled roots reach down
to batten on my shin.

This side the wall is mobile, motley, lit
by hours that keep the clock, handwriting hours
that spell: confirm the tickets, cut the grass,
order the books, put air in the tires, wash hair,
get Jill's address, have Hattie polish the silver,
make will . . .

Make way. All I can leave is the wall
(the blotter, the photographs, the bicycle), my shelter
between laps of living, my address.

Should I be gone
(tomorrow, perhaps, I will not answer the phone),
think of me not as graceless, but as grown
whole in my tongue. And should you pass,
between hours, through your wall of grass,
iron, and oak, here where my quiet work
runs like small waters under the pared light
that swallows love,
here we could speak.

## Glimpses of the Moon

Where has the moon been? For many years now
(the middle years in the city) I have thought of her
along with Christmas stories, gingerbread
men, and immortal dogs that were somehow shockingly buried
by the three pines—also with extempore
effusion—as a thing not to be put by but
to solve, to discipline by counter-light.

But because they sold the herd on the twenty-ninth,
and are starting the President's house the first of the month,
and this is the last September I can pace
the pasture-road in private, here I have come
to watch the moon climb
over Dead Man to the locust tip and down
Huffman's tin sheds toward Salem.

And it is hard to believe
in ashy beauty, hard to believe in the blood
childishly moved by explicable light, hard to believe
this access to the Barrens circles back
to Long Quarter, cones in the winter fire,
a child without a desire that could not be met
by pond, fern, Bible story, poem, or sunset
freely dispensed, and fur's and feather's comfort.
I have later thought
of loves denatured and unmagicked, thought
of Astolat and Ida in the moon's teeth,
and Lear unquartered on the windy heath.

                        And thought
suddenly vanishes, and I am met
by fullness in the bristling field, wider awake
than words or false footstep. The furious birds
are silent, and the moon-
rainbow through watered clouds leaps up, and the pious
blood that was hidden
beats a hymn-tune for its sisters ridden
by bulls, its sailors driven,
its sons set mother-naked on the kingdom,
for all God's quarry of rain, maze, and oven.
Beats beyond explanation how chastity
rides, huntress and queen, in our roads to be our token.
For the child

in the blood born mild
comes walking, comes returning
over the flood field, on the first road, comes burning
the bones' map of this valley.

     Oh may I
turn at cold morning to quarter crossing
the Great Road taken, remembering
among bird cries and the ways to work the rising
of the real light in love of the forsaken
fields and walk my widow's weeds
rightly in praising.


## DA CAPO

Go back. In the first breathing-place, Lector,
there was a garden, bellied big with fruit,
and gorgeous stalks of amaranth to pluck,
the love-lies-bleeding pigweed, purple pranked
and fat with praise. And, Abba, it was good,
sun-singing, in the elegance of hours
moving processional to moony peace.
Till frost-fall. Till the powdery mildew.
Till Adamo at evening lost his way,
and it was rusty where the rose had blown,
and, barren-breast, he cursed the barren thorn,
and every bleating beast in fickle Eden.

Go back the long way round red man, the way
Magellan took, and Christoph, for a dream.
Item: mine eye organic is a form
in darkness got, along the nine-times night,
to meet invisible America.
Else why, else why birth-breaking, exile's track,
narrow night-watch at ship's prow? Circle back,
faint sailor. Weep. Long bones into the sand
witness, and ashes where the firebush burned.

Back, pauvre palmer. Late in wounds I speak:
it is of roses and of rust to make
the rustless rose. Of Adam to create
the major man, the comer. He will die.
Bloom, roses of his blood. I garner you.
It is a garden, Abba. It is new.

Plainer, it is to be inseparate,
thought sailing always from the Belle Patrie.
To plant France in the wilderness. To know
we are at home in Québec, speaking so
these syllables of love in the old tongue.

This care of things, their scant becoming light,
it is of this, childheart, to darkly speak.
Their glint upon the glasses of my eye,
a kindling, say a kenning of that face
all fiery, bright in every bourne of space
and after-space, burning in every time
and in before and after. It is free.
It is the music of the mind, or say
the poem of the mind, without a word.
It is the speech that Caesar made a sword,
Vincent a flower, Francis a homely bride.
It is one speech. I stand in a sunsquare
all dusty from a mountain. It is there,
Pisan, in marble. Johann, it is here,
your chord across the garden. It is where
we fall, dark Paul, dust eye into the dust,
and raise the shape of fire, face to face.

FROM *The Farewells* (1981)

## Departure

Where is the emperor, where is the clown,
where is the great-haired lady? Stone.

Where is the bird that purchased here
on mossy head and marble gear
mistaking quarry for the bough?

I hear his crazy vespers now
for grace and guard, the double call
along the shadowy groves at Coole
bidding the sycamores farewell.
                    Farewell.


## The Sycamores at Satyr Hill

Our settlers on the valley floor
between the ridges, rank and file
like gray Confederates light
this February sundown white.

No match for birches, proudly down
from Massachusetts, or for Towsontown
moving like Stonewall eastward to consume
Sherwood's and Merrick's and my farm.

It is a colder cause, but still the cry
"Sic semper." What if graybeards die,
council and cavalry undo
pippin and minnow?

How is it then with Beauty? She survives
in rocky holds that energy will kill
and we be cast reliant on the sill
of space, no Adonais
beckoning, only rock and stone and star
to ravage. Cold war
casualties, cold as the will
that severed soul from earth, and severs still.

## Another Part of the County

1

Here, where dogs learn
to set, or to lay down,
and the motorcycles roll
Friday to Sunday over Hartley Mill,
where Creeping Charlie threads the lawn,
and Grumman lobbies for a Light Industrial zone,

between lives, in a pause
of August sycamore, immobile before storm,
while words and wheels run over and run down
all that we know of form, I feel
like the last Indian, squat on Wissahickon
schist, the year
they chartered this fair county, all the way
from Susquehanna to the hills. No room
for Minckus.

      "His brow
two yards, his arrow
five quarters, headed with a splinter,
white, in the form of a heart."

A white stone splinter. They have asked me to shoot
the water moccasin, his head
in the form of a heart.

2

The bones of our ancestors, Andaste, did you know
they could die?
When you moved over Blue Ridge on your thigh
three-quarter yards, they were already dead,
Maize Mother, the Great Raven that was God,
gone down before the pendulum, the glass,
the *Discourse:* Great Pan,
libidinous pastor, stopped in marble skin.
A heavy portage, the ancestral children.

3

Eagle, the edge of time
is always falling. We are nothing fit
to mourn, mere green
life. Already at my back
the metal men are marching. Bear and Goat,
Lion and Maiden crack. The Bull,

last at the salt lick, heaves his muzzle
skyward. Thunder-bird,
on steely wings, from circumpolar
forays, fire eyes
aflash, breaks cover.
Grass is over.


## Naming the Gunpowder Falls

There are several theories. Refugees from the Plot
is one of them—not likely. My favorite
has the Indians planting a packet
of gift grains on the river bank. They failed to sprout.

Now any self-respecting Piscataway,
learned in simples, fish-heads
under his corn, his fecund squash
botching the Governor's garden, knew better than that.

So tell me, shaman, how the canny tribe
whose land I inhabit (cave, crude arrowhead
remain) came to soil-sowing
the crop red Adam also set in clay
across the Bay—
Salamis, Hohenlinden, Leningrad—
when he spat out his seed.


## Matchman

A burner born, I eye
the tin of gasoline
and the out-travelled tire
that, filled, will fire
the brush-pile damp with spring
and creatures gendering.

Who stole the brand (they tell)
lit paradise and hell—
all that our hands could raise
to the delighted skies,
all that our hands could wreck
for bleeding freedom's sake.

Whether it's sentiment,
the last titanic thread,
or some less lenient
link to the frightful dead
dogs of our throughways, downed
counties, and slicked
pinions, my hand
is tethered. Princely, I
appoint my neighbor's son
my devilish deputy.
Thus heaven's wars are won,
who lifts no mortal blade
but grass, which at his word
flames on and on.


## Hardwood Country

1
Octobre, cadenza. One would always know,
in this rude land, these colors and their close,
the Indian pomes, Valhalla's roofs ablaze,
poet and peasant in the glow of things
reading of earth and sky the finite rhymes.

2
Professor Coleridge, the Professor
of Creative Languages: if you begin
with a rhyme, you have to end with one.
Because the ear expects, the eye, the hand,
a repetition in the finite mind
of the first word, eternal seed
(or fifty words, that bring but one to bear):
marigold, maple, dogwood, liquidambar.

3
Professor James, the Professor
of Moral Science: intensely enough
imagined, all your characters go free,
bog, wood, and wayside; Adirondack glory:
a world upon a word, and it is red,
hot Dido's coronet, gray Duncan's bed.

4
Newes form the New Founde Lande: we thanked
God for this tapestry. No loom
could match it, never Turkey, never Tyre
rugged, robed, or tented like the living dyer
princes of blood: viburnum, burning bush,
a sumac candle to a summer wish,
or Judas April making. Who knows how
the grass recovers when the fall is done?
When Michael sentry turns the future all
to flame, we rise to red occasion.

5
So, sourwood, a skint and vital thread.
So, tupelo, great thigh and golden head.
So, wasted Ilion, that burned for Greece,
Hekabe helled, and winter in the house
of all but poetry, whose haut amens
skitter to sleep beside the evergreens.

## THE TRACKERS

Hounds I have never seen run in my dream
down schist and shale where I have never been
on Hershfield's Hill, bursting the laurel cover,
rounding oak roots. I hear them over and over.
Some farm a mile away
must loose them. There is nothing there by day.

And what do they sing, with their bell voices,
soft eyes, strained haunches
unleashed in the night wood?
Dream-blood, dream-blood.

Not mine, for I am not the quarry.
It is something I carry, dear-life, down
outcrop, leaf bed,
side-split, but saviour-footed.

And I
fall, piecemeal—
tooth, tongue, nail—but they cannot feast
on my pawky bones, on my breast
strings, for the prize is sped

from my arms into waking
day, into jay
scream, and the house wren
stuttering into the bent
windrow. And Hershfield's low
Sinai is silent.

This is a darker dream than day can discover,
homebred, mother to mother, sire to daughter,
sharper than sin: the houndstooth of the lover.


## Album Leaves

*for my brother at 50*

1
There we are
nude in the bath house. Mary Brown
is towelling our toes.
And there we are
on a stone wall with Daddy.
(Where was that?
Biddeford? Blue Ridge Summit?)
And there he is
in skirts, with a hobbyhorse.
Someone we never knew
but pretend we do.

Who's this? Miss Ramsdell would ask, holding up the text,
and covering up the legend. And we said
Henry-the-Seventh-who-built-a-strong-Treasury.
We got A.

And this? It must be great-grandmother
whose maiden name we forget, whom none alive
could name without the label. Her matron's eyes
look mildly out at us, the future.

And oh yes!
that was my orange snowsuit, I'm sure it was.
I can feel it now, soggy as all get-out,
pure wool, strapped under the boot,

too intricate to shed
without maternal aid.

The Yearbook photo. I was seventeen
with a permanent. How could I know
I would never see Nancy again,
or Helen, or Amy's Joe
lost in the Philippines? I had plans, too,
which did not include glasses, tenure, or living 22
years longer than Shelley. Once I biked
to Lerici, a foolish thing to do
on that coast. But, as the guidebook says, "the view
is very recommended."

2
Views. Remember Elephant Rock,
domed poll and back
rising above the tide? From one blue glass
on Aunt Louisa's table, I can get
completely around her house. I still end up
at the Harvard Classics—brave new names they were,
then: Aristotle, Schopenhauer.
Girl in a wicker chair, a scene of the self. "The picture
of the mind revives again," but only the picture.
The mind is here with us, composing, quarrying
old summer silences. The tide
rises and falls. Do you remember the smell
of the clam flats? I remember, but no more
keenly than I can hear
the conversation of dreams: we waded, spoke
words that were histories without a book
to save them, unless we
are the book we cannot read,
dark documents of seasons with the dead.

3
Never again
can we climb Chocorua for the first time. Tiers of eyes
mount to its skinny tip like trees,
some perishing for want of light.
I thought of it the other night—
Aunt Katie Codman's garden, Indian Leap,
old William James, scanning the level lake: "and the islands
also hang together at . . . bottom"; "our several minds
plunge to the reservoir." And shall we there

find Brownie, and the six lost weeks he took
getting to Frederick?
I have the farmer's postcard in my book:
R. Randall, Baltimore. *Dear Sir,
have stray, your name on collar.* Every day,
even of a dog's life, would fill
a library. It cannot, thus, be time we read,
the every feather in a sparrow's head,
the every name (Adam) upon the collar, when we come
breathless, back to the bottom.

4
Nouns (third declension) ending in -n,
-ur, -us, -e, -al, -ar,
and *caput* are neuter. Sargon II,
Sennacherib, Esarhaddon, and Assurbanipal. I never had trouble
understanding *The Waste Land*. Much is lost
I would recall, and what remains behind
a cabinet of wonders, called the Mind.
In that conditioned gallery air,
musing upon my father's wreck, I stare
at lapidary curios, skull and thorn,
a narwhal tusk marked Unicorn
(so the guard said
"I didn't think they really existed"), stare
at a blue mantle trimmed in vair
"for a lady" (but the lady isn't there),
at the orange snowsuit.

                              Where,
then, if not in store, and not a thing,
is our continuing? Meaning
makes in us like the light that breaks
the mists on Snowdon when we bring
Helvellyn to it, and Chocorua,
and Horeb, and the quip
of an old codger underneath the rock
where Gladstone (1892) harangued his flock: "Ewart
always had a loud voice." Many musics, Glaslyn, make
my song, but mute
by Rothay sleeps the poet,
no postlude written, self forgot
in silent darkness, or in silent light.

5
                              "*Use* your death,"
said James, aged 28. But what use can
so daily an adventure prove? Love must undress,
at last, the "personal effects" be carted off
to the Carry-On Shop. My Bean's size 3
boots will fit no one in the family. And what was meant
by the collection? Kenneth making stew
at 13, rue de Savoie. "You've
got to build it on the meat." Indeed you do.
It was too cold to keep your feet
on that floor. When the chauffage failed, we took a stall at the
     Comique
and jogged home out of breath
across the Pont-Neuf.
How shall I use that death?

6
Spun on a double thread? They bring the news
from Genesis: we replicate by twos.
But still, we do not share our parents' views.

This view, then, from the bridge (Jan. '76)
over the rising branch, reminds me: I must mix
more cornmeal for the birds; that Mother, though she'd recognize
the corner-cupboard, never saw my house, and does not see
my house, having left her eyes,
quite properly, to Hopkins, to some second
seer of winter water and thin skies
flagging beyond the skeletons of trees, like skies
I Magic Markered in my *Coloring Book*
*of the Middle Ages;* you said
my blues were not authentic.

                    This flood
will smash the watergate again; we can
"build but accidental fences," says the *Final*
*Impressions of a Psychical Researcher;* can but stare
at the nuthatch jogging down the sycamore
in his hard-hat.

              How to bless—
we don't know that. Of suffering
we know something: the child's cry
of separation tunes us till we die. Of sacrifice

this little: brothers all, who lay
leaf over leaf, to leafless clarity.


## Outliving

It is not what they think. You go some twenty years
behind your mother till the day she dies. Some twenty more,
in secret, in the thin disguise
of childlessness, divorce, and a career,
you follow her.
There are some clues; your sister
is one of them—the pretty one,
homemaker, and man's woman;
every shoe in its bag, and all of them clean.

I am the half that lived deep down.
My body is taking me there, but I will come
down with a difference. At sixty-nine,
I am in a place my mother has never been.
I may make seventy, seventy-five,
and not a soul alive
to scout me. I must make shift
in this dispensation, finally free
to foot it, shoeless as I came,
into my life, her gift.


## Family Portraits

### Nature
I am Nature. They have always loved me, but not
in the flesh. They take my picture,
they like that; their walls
are full of me. The worst thing
about your children is their affection.
They will give me a handsome funeral,
all eulogies and Bach. They will say
I am happier someplace else—"above."
My face will haunt them, but it will not be
the face of love.

MIND
I am the Mind. My address
is Limbo, where three roads cross.
I am a tree, a goose,
a bay. I am a house
and you are in it.

BEAUTY
I am the odd one. I
have never come out. I am shy,
unlike my elder sister—too familiar,
some say. I don't know;
she's always been nice to me. She has so many
kids, I don't need any of my own,
except, of course, my dream-children.

JUSTICE
I am the ugly duckling. For a while
they tried pigtails; then they bobbed my hair.
Nothing would work. My mother was despair,
my father outrage. Gracie
lent me some lipstick. I bought heels
and a bikini. Nothing would do;
no one will ever marry me. I read
I might have turned quite beautiful in bed.
I read a lot. "My skin is black but oh my soul is white,"
I read that. Is it true?
Dudie won't tell me. He's in college now.

TIME
We were orphans, a large family. They look to me
as the head; I provide
as best I can. They begin
to question my authority. They have forgotten
the home farm—Father, Mother,
and Alma, who died young.
I miss her.

SOUL
Though born of high estate, I wed
a wealthy farmer's son. We were never happy.
I began to dream
about the castle. Once I wrote a letter.
It was returned—that's just like my father.
He was good to his men. I was an only daughter. I have three.

Faith is strong as an ox; Hope
is the moony one; and Charity,
when she grows up, will be handsome.

PAIN
I am a mystery. In the flesh
Brébeuf saw me, and Joan, and Christ.
I did not surprise them. I surprise the hare.

When Love surprised me, I put on
godhead and ghost. All lovers
see me: Tristan,
broken Lautrec, blind Paul. All women
call me. My name
is Pain. I answer prayer.

FORM
They never found a cure for me; they tried
everything: the bomb,
drugs, sainthood, even compulsory
sterilization (it comes to the same thing). They computed
the brain, slicked the salt marshes, burned the grain,
and sat there, counting their wages. They never knew
where I came from, who
employed me, when
I was going to die. If they thought
they'd got me, I'd crop out
someplace else. I do not love
my fine hosts, though there's always been a few
who think I do. They may die
unrequited. I like graves too.


# STRATFORD, O.

Jetstream, fluorocarbon, slick—the wreck
of landscape, marriage, the north sea,
earth, air, and water—a tiresome story
written at Genesis, before the cause
was any poison in us.

It is the poison—beware the cup!—
that sets the hero piping in the play.
It is the poison that we can see
sickening the skin of dreary Canada.

And who would think, from so severe a state
of harmony, to drive the Dene for bread
and letters from the warm
herds and the undivided
waters? Who would think
Abaddon thoughts, to give the maids to drink
madness, and mothers in the oily dark
tree dreams and southern fancies, devil's work?

And him, the master of our revels, here
transported like the very tongue to speak
angelic flights—what scuffle in the lane
schooled him in murderous ambition,
lust, envy, and—yes—love, the poet's scheme
for players? Wary of
our plaudits, jack and king and lady all
shake hands with us at Stratford in the hall.


## THE MAN WHO MADE A RIVER

Brilliant, the river runs
between hills where the light shifts
on tuffy greens and purples; little rocks
spark and go dull. It pours at you, vivider
than the Salmon, than a dream.
It is under the dome
of the Art Institute of Chicago.

They do not make rivers like that any more,
not even in France
where the great bears dance
on the cave walls, sealed away from their bones.

Shall we dance (take hands), shall we dance, Snake and St. John,
steed Nancy, red Brandy, retriever of rain?
Shall we dance in a ring,
under the skylight, on a day of storm,
here by old flat-foot gray Lake Michigan?


## GIVERNY

Bearded to match his willows, he sits here
by his pond. It is always summer. Far away

ice cracks the jetties, holy towers fall,
the Channel rages. Let the world be done.

In the quiet of the lilies, never won
since Eden rose and the archangel fell,
that battle with the light goes on and on.


## R. VAN R.

Old pudgy-face, I like your negatives,
the space a shadow takes,
the bible blacks and whites.

                        What other lens
could tender dailiness—a lace,
a lamp, a sill—or stylus trace
how Saskia slept, how Jesus prayed,
the mortal sky above his head
no-color, but a lightning stroke
from helm to halter glancing back
to where the darkness has no weight?
Is that a cousin, carpenting?
In Tobit's house, is that a wing?


## CUMAE

There are two doors here, according to the story,
both leading out of sunlight into gold
of a different sort, treasure of a different sort.
Trees that have grown in darkness, blooming light,
come by the cave-mouth, where even the bats are silent.
Here comes the hero, craving the late voices
of friends, of fathers, those who dreamed this shore,
but blind in sight of it, looked earlier
upon the fields where (some say) flowers ply,
and others, fires. The hero enters.

The temple door, where come
the people out of the punishing sun
of these regions, stands open.
Under a roof of gold
a craftsman, it is told, put off his wings

of wax, the conversation of queens,
old crimes, old voyages, and all the freight
of vengeance in the provinces. Of these
he made, in memory, stone images.
But one
he could not master, and his hands dropped down
and emptied, for his son
lay, failing artifice, on the seafloor,
dumb to his hand, deaf to the temple whore.

## A Farewell to Music

There is a time for meeting lords of time,
as father, brother, lover, muse, and friend,
in single combat; times when the mind,
learning itself like muscles, separates
thighs, fingers, diaphragm,
substance and dream.

This is self-time, the oracle that speaks
decision at the crossroads doubly heard,
once in the sequence of the royal bed,
once in the right-of-way cleared by the sword.

Last, at Colonus, when the catalog
is near complete, and we forget
whose *Grosse Fugue* this is—Mozart,
Beethoven?—and the performer,
whoever he is, repeats the ingenious
dovetailed design, at last there come
the rooks to silence him, the shelter
of this old grove, this sacred nine
moving like music in the stream,
one choir that rose on Kithairon
abandoned of all kings but one.

## The Soloist

He must be a fine fellow, although we
have never seen him. "Look,"
cries the Martyr, and we
look. "Rescue" (the Mariner), and we row.

"Read" (the inglorious Milton), and we pen
our student names inside his book.

Your highland solitary dabs a dye
upon his sheep; your Crusoe craves his kind;
your cells their multiples; your Cain
his brother come again.

                    We cannot dream,
from Adam on, a solo dream, but one:
a dream of dying, alien
to our last blood, so unoriginal to the end,
"Father" (it cries), "and Friend."

## FALLING ASLEEP IN CHAPEL

It is morning by the clock. Under the dark,
where the loose hound bays night
on Dead Man, and the cooped cock
sleeps staring,
the field-bones crack with spring.
Palm, plume, blade, and tongue
swell in the valley's skin; waters awake
for Christ's sake, fools of light
rising, come in a night,
come in a night and gone,
temple and vine,
child after child, and man,
after his swollen stem
has seeded up the sky,
man gone. And I
come to this empty house,
glad of an iron sun
falling on sterile stone,
to listen to what I am.

I am loud all ways. Man
and woman in my skull,
too constant in their vows,
beget such prodigies—
ark, orchard, arrow, and nail,
and swaddling-band and shroud,

the star on the hill, and the flail
in the crowd crop—such crew
from one incestuous bed,
I swear I have begun
all heaven and its blue
weathers in my god-head.
Look where Leviathan
bleeds on my hook, exhausted.

But oh it is I
die, and it is my
daughter plucks out, on my porch, and my knee
cramps into stone. And in a sudden
silence like a load
of water without world,
deep in my diving skin,
deeper than light can come,
I feel flesh grip on my blood bone,
grip, and go down.

        And I am
nothing, man unmade,
rockroot, driftweed,
before the dream began
of walking in a name.
It is as if a voice
but wordless as a hand
grew in my greening stuff. As if horizon,
Virginia, and coasts
of stars grew in the eyes
I have not got, and land
rose and brought forth my feet,
and after that . . .

The dream dies, and I wake
Adam, in Christ's name's sake,
Adam newly begun,
ribbed with creation. See,
my knees pray, my lungs move
mounds of tall air. I stare
into the iron sun. I warm. I walk
into the nightfall spring
from his hand, king
of red clay land, lord of our issuing

into the bone valley,
virgin and bright as day, a spy
of all light-rising
ghosts in the god-net.

May his seal set
friendly in flesh unite
us for he is
master of dreaming day, and grave
governor of lily
and sparrow, and the soul set
on righteousness, the last
thing we can do, being too
trying in all pride,
wound-wide
proof of the father and fall.
May all
his sons of the Eastertide
bearing walk clean-breathing
into the wings of his kingdom.


## Eve Enters Heaven

Alone I walked. Wherever I went
I was the oldest woman. After me
none motherless.

I enter as I entered then
earth-minted
mother of murders.

I come clean
of apple promises. I listen
all ways, but the wingy
orchards are dumb
save for shameless sparrows.

Mine again
birdsong, and mine
every mother and risen son.

## A Child Enters Heaven

I heard them tell me sleep,
my fever dropped
and all my dreams stood up.

How can my room hold them?
They are a town
where I have never been, a mountain.
How do I know this street,
sailsheet, wolf pack, water
that I breathe under?

Wake, they told me.
All my dreams lay down.
Names of things unknown
came to me friendly
and I speak with them
as I were grown.


## The Blind Schoolmaster Enters Heaven

I saw what words see with their eyes,
the haunted girls and marching boys,

saw what the deaf harper sang
in Hesiod's or David's tongue,

saw Hades, and unholy light,
fire Breadstreet and fire Cripplegate

and wonder how I see the sun
unenvied, at the end of night,
who took so long the light for dark,
the dark for light.


## A Puritan Enters Heaven

I said to my eyes, so far. Harrow
this row. Tomorrow
we shall play at hide-and-seek under the grape arbor.

Tomorrow, I said to my ears, we shall sing
how Jack the Journeyman
and the princess in the tower

rhymed as hoofbeats, rode—
I said to my arms and legs,
my arms about her waist,
my lips in her hair—

to a leafy place in the sun
and there, deed done,
white kine without a fence
will watch us dance.


## A Mariner Enters Heaven

The gates of Hercules were not for me.
I was a sailor on a different sea
and watched the furrow widening behind
toward all my wealth of body and of mind.

Singular shapes, how did I come to share
your haunts with any salt adventure?
Lub feet, house fingers, and an eye
for flowers want a field to steer by.

Some devil of a dreamer, heaven-bent
or hell-bent—what's the difference at home?—
impressed me, and I went
those savage leagues to satisfy a whim.

That wake should widen at contrary prow
toward the lost villages—I wonder now
I did not trust my captain or his mate
to spring the latchet on my father's gate.


## The Prodigal Enters Heaven

I never went back. That was my father's story,
what he might have done had I come crawling
stubbled and stinking to his tree.
I sailed away.

I hiked the universe.
I was free,

built bridges, hawked in the provinces, was paid,
slept with honey women in the shade
of boughs no sandy man could dream,
saw snowy children leaping in a stream,
hungered, but not for home.

Aging, I found a father in my face
and did not love him, rusty man
that he was, not even for childhood's sake.
But then my tongue, his make
and rebel, trimmed my youth
and age of fable. Then it spoke
home truth.


## A Whole Man Enters Heaven

The first thing that I noticed was
everyone had his health.
Nobody dreamed
of murder or a wife.

Here side by side
the Roman couches and the Mormons stride
and time is patched. No sentries keep the lane,
no stewards measure the lord's grain.

All discipline is lifted. You might say
I was unemployed—but let me tell you
there are more histories than I can ever know
to enter into; all my limbs and eyes
and spirits that reported paradise
in temporal perspective grow
boundless; all my mind
works without end.


## Salvation Kit

We have wondered, going to sleep, whatever to take
should fire break out. Priorities are plain:

the children, the dogs, the work. And after that
clothes, I expect. The things we brought
into this world, or needed to be decent. In the event
I suppose we should snatch whatever was near to hand:
the front-hall bowl, the family umbrella stand.

If I should die before I wake
(we have also wondered, tossing with backache)
and my soul, like the soul of a house, consume
or be caught naked, either it must fly
like cinders to the mourner's eye
whose tears a little while remind
but wash in nearer waters blind
to that old mansion and its shades,

                or it must cower
cold in its deeds, while even its longings
burn.

I have known a beggar, but only in a dream,
wonder, as at a tongue of flame, to hear
the voice of emptiness command: Take up
your staff, and go barefoot
to a green place in family land. Fear not.
Carry an empty cup.


## DEGENERATION

You can let things go. Coons and mildew
will do the work. Three years it took
the squirrels to finish the blanket
in the back room. A quarter-century
for the roof to fall in.
Floods, dozers, thunderbolts
give quicker results. You can swamp ten yachts
off Fastnet, or knock up a block
of Baltimore, and not a pot to tell
what dinner was, who cooked there, or how well.

Reverse creation
should start with man, provided the sages
figured it right
and God abides his meter.

But the plan, as I see it, is neater.
Oil moves on the face of the water.
Heaven and earth are undivided.
The beetle sits in the bush,
the lion lies by the fish,
the clearcut hill slips down,
dark covers the ruined town. A naked man,
the mock of Adam, moves
his last lips as the full
fire whips a molten tide
to his ribs, where the first bride
burns. No names
names he, his tongue
gone with the grass, the world behind his eyes
a burning glass.


## JILL UPON LOVE & LANGUAGE

Now language has come down to earth,
it proves no second birth. Naming of parts
in love, or laboratory arts,
is common speech.

I need no man to teach
me cherry lips and fronts of pearl.
Who loves not Goldilocks, dear girl? Regrets
not Galahad the unspoiled knight?
Who dreams not red while lying white?

But what of those who by the sword
between, or sea, or mental fight,
outsleep both beauty and the beast
to touch original at last

the stuff that Dian made a light,
who's pocky cinder by the news,
and Jack and Jill gone gray—all those
who keep an undegraded eye
and tongue to tell a master by?

## The Bird That Sang Mozart

This bird that sang one day
from every living tree
in my lot, and next door—
I've never heard him before,
or since; could not catch sight of him.
He is not in Peterson.

According to what he sang
he is in *The Magic Flute*.
I wrote it note for note
on the shopping list, like so:
"Der Vogelfänger bin ich ja,
sing ho, sing heisa hopsasa,"
till all the wood was opera—what else could it be?
A tad Caruso in a walnut tree,
a bird that catches birds caught me
with a cage on my back, and turned me free.

Shall we meet again? I do not think so.
I do not revisit Canada, Mexico,
or concerts, even the *Messiah*.
I shall not walk with Mozart; that is not what he meant.
But the Hershfields' Christmas pines are different,
visited, musicked as an antique grove
where randy God assaulted mortal love
in rustic shape, and both disguises met,
once only, and a future was begot—
some oaf, some yokel, rapt in the boneyard
by airy callings in his bastard blood.


## Continuum

In a wood, I was sad
for an old farm dead; cowshed
collapsing over picinics, no homestead.

They did not move in a hurry; the Park
claimed them; they took
every beam, every brick or stone (no one
remembers, though they aren't twenty years gone).
But they left the garden, all the bulbs,

the wisteria root, the yews
grown monstrous, the day lilies.
I saw a woman, against the law,
digging them, leaving the ground raw.

And I think as I plant,
unearthing nails and bottles, lids, short lead
pipes and green mottled marbles, how we tenant
time, too. For my house may stand
another hundred years, or the vines I fight
take it before the City, or Joppatowne
come with its trowels to take the jonquils home.
We can change places, but a place
for all our compositions plays ground-base.

But what of hours, what space
do they take? where does music heard
harbor, or a child's face? Here an iris,
there a footpath is witness, but of limbs'
labor, as the letter
keeps of the spent
mind trace, without element.

A bird sings, "Frederick, Frederick," as I work
in leaves, and in unsent
letters, dinner, Troy.
In Chios what bird sang, when Homer was a boy?
Or in Annapolis,
Grandmother, mute to me,
what mandrake voice cried, "Children, home for tea!"?


## Touchstones

Here is the stone like a hatchet, here is the stone like a heart,
not beautiful, but young. At nine or ten
I salvaged them from where they lay—
brook, pathway—I've forgotten,
but not far from the start.

Now I've grown an eye
for pebbles: the more abstract
the better, grained ones
from the mountains, smooth ones from the sea. And useful too
to bed narcissus. But, you know,

I could never identify them, as I could Abou
ben Adhem, Donuil Dhu.

                    Have you
played Desert Island lately, what you'd take
for the inner man—your Beethoven, your Blake,
your Bible? Absolutely free
choice, guaranteed to make
a cultivated Crusoe. I'm not sure.
Lars Porsena, who by the Nine Gods swore
of Clusium—he'd come. The sands of Dee.
And Hohenlinden, when the sun was low.
And in the silence, singing on the track
to the home of my fathers, no gods,
but they'd welcome me back.

## An Elegy of Sorts

Some never take farewells. I speak
of solids: the three-cornered chair,
the andirons, the wood-barrel, things that pass
from house to family house, like the rocker
of applewood I bought in the repair
shop in Parkville, pegged and bent
in some farm shed or Appalachian
kitchen, sold up by the children.
Owner to owner, rent to rent
they pass, the ranks of the indifferent
dumb angels, those who feed,
comb, cover, decorate, and entertain
our final love, the flesh, so handy made
to vanish. Oh I pray
them daily: give us bread
and pans to bake it.
Bless, four saints, this bed
and sheets to make it.
In my voice I pray
these inarticulate (they do) to stay.

And in my silence pray for tongues
of men and angels at the pass
where language falls

and none escapes who tells
what love becomes, or dogs, or daffodils.


## THE WHITE RHINOS

They are not white, but gray, like those they call
black. They have a square lip, or "wide,"
for grazing. They are mild.
And now, at Meru, there are only five.

Of this great lummox, the skin horn is all
that's taken, to be rendered as a dust
most potent in the pharmacy of lust.

For pleasure and for poacher's purse
they died, whose names first burst our tongue:
Behemoth, and Leviathan.
Reason followed, also love—
an odd configuration of
forces, this.
Which one will miss us, when we miss?


## THE KINGFISHER, FEBRUARY

The fishing is a little thin,
my friend, but what can I provide?
You scorn my seed, my love of the late night
on snow, where cardinal and jay
oppose the prospect of a world gone white.

What do you see
from the sycamore, the edge of your patrol
on Long Green Branch? You feed
on fry I could not catch; you breed
in burrows four feet long I could not build;
you fly; you rattle. We are different-skilled,
even for the same back yard. The barbecue
is useless as a rose to you.

Of planets, then.
Should there be birds or angels, beasts or men,
pine trees or pignuts? Scant imagining,

that tongues should be, or eyes, or they be fed
by what we are fed:
blue, yellow, red,
minnows in millstreams, sunflower seed.

Behind the eye, the mind makes images,
but not of things, but yet conformed to things
as kingfisher to angel, borrowed light.
Out in the dark
fast fading you, my diver, what dread beings,
or brotherly, die daily to our sight?


## Arrival

It is good, after a Grand Tour
of all the continents, to be back
in New England, winter coming on,
the garden put to bed, things in their naked
lineaments, only the juniper
as ever, gray-blue,
green-blue against the once and future snow.

It is good to light the fire, good to know
the hutch of home. Let Mozart play
the hopsasa, a quaint geometry
of motion. Sit still. Listen.
It is the Good, lost mère. Her note:
please wake me. Her dishevelled hair
from sleep. "How late," and then, "how lean
you have grown, soldiering."

So, so,
Ewige. And yet
it is fat, Virginia. Our kin, their tale,
the orchards . . . Ja,
the melons in their clay.

How prodigal the fire. His way
to fat this evening of your sere rentrée.

How many tongues are weary. *Wir wandelten
durch Feuergluten . . . die vor Liebe
brennen.*

How good to hear you singing.

FROM *Moving in Memory* (1987)

## Middle Age, Middle East

I am Piedmont born and bred
between far hills and sea,
great hardwoods overhead,
and waters gently
falling down to the Bay.

Sometimes at winter dawn
a bank of cloud will look
like the Blue Ridge or Green,
and I am yester-drawn
over, or north, or south
along the scouting path.

Or August evenings when
the sycamores go still,
my flat east-running brook
slaps at my father's keel
in salt illusion. Home
is where dogwood, mayapple
and bloodroot know my name,
or I know theirs. Perhaps
we're both adventureless,
and how we cross or come
native, the same.


## The Clearing

There are some birds—thrasher, chat—
that love a tangle. We've got that
in Maryland, as in any state
with honeysuckle. There are some
birds love a stump, a riddled bole,
a rot-rich windfall. Even so
the farmer thinks I'm crazy not to clear
my woodlot for the fire.
Clear, clear, clear
call philosophe and forester, and clear
call psychologue and surgeon. And I clear
an acre (some birds like a lawn)

but leave the rest
more or less natural. Here in the east
there's no place hasn't been
ploughed, timbered, quarried, left at length to ruin,
no place nemesis
won't repossess.

If gardens were the aim,
gardens there might have been
with hawthorn hedge-rows, wild hawk-hills,
and wild-rice wetlands; seasoning trees,
reflecting rivers near to town,
some tangle to remember, some old plot
where hell-bent boys trespassed, and the hermit
thrush from piney cover
sang lover after lover
asleep, sang hunting father
high to the ridge, where cloud
obscured the face but not the hand of God.

Oh quaint Algonquian
dream of deer and plover!
The nightmare darkening over
this new-found land is called the dream
Dominion. It has no master.
Equal in its vise
our disenchanted works and days depend
upon the machinations of a mind
cleared of its match in earth or skies. Nightwatch
is violent. It always was, but then
the wind- or wing-struck quarry lived again,
and every April fleeced the field with green. We woke
to ancient fellowship, daydream
of roots immortal as the sun.

What shall restore
cedar and sycamore, sweet springs,
the secrets of the forest floor, where now
backhoes and scaffoldings
and gray computers set us free
to manufacture loves and lifeless things
along the steely groves where no bird sings?

## Thunder

The beagle is under the bed, and the mixed
poodle goes terrified, but the old deaf
terrier licks his paws
peacefully in the kitchen.
He is seventeen and impervious
to his fleas, or traffic, or rut.
Most senses are shut. I think maybe his eyes
are failing—hard to tell when he keeps his nose
and goes for his walk unerring: the usual stops,
the usual divagations—Welsh's porch,
Gregg's stoop, the compost pile.
On good days he can go a quarter mile.

I too fear the flash and the clap
that will knock out the stove and the well
pump, but I keep the oil lamp
trimmed, like a wise professor, against the day
of the power failure. What does the beagle fear?
She has never been struck, never missed a meal.
The water is fresh in her bowl; her single
misdemeanor (being found in the Charleston chair)
she repeats and repeats,
smiling at empty threats.

*Timor mortis* it could not be.
It is more like *terror mundi*. Once we hid
under rock, under wood. But we learned to defy
the unknown enemy, piled high
his temples, and drank blood
to silence him. Old Thunderhead,
we called him, and we danced
and sang in painted faces, beating drums.

The beagle finds her secret catacombs; the terrier will die
easy in his afflictions, walking
into his senseless ground without a word
of protest, ward of an absurd
keeper of kibble pails, a well-provided
flea-market god, a cutter of nails, a comber
of burrs: seventeen years
at home, a steady path,
a stubborn humor, and a perfect faith.

## Grackles

The grackles gather, loud in leaves yet green
but paling before fire
consumes them, and still winter
compounds of leavings yet another garden.

So black thoughts (we would have them) fly
and May's recourse how many centuries
has solaced with a garland on the brow
of violets and daisies.

How marvellous, how pat
our rousing recollections and our slant
rhymes for the rounding seasons. Small comfort
the rainbow hummer after honey bent,

the rose unfurling on the thorny shoot,
the rest in nature, or the rest in art—
two glasses that look glassy out
and alter nothing.

                Is it out of fashion
to crack the Arctic and the Argentine
vistas, to cheer
migrants who braved a barrier
reef, or a river face, to win
clear of the causeways some unseasoned coast
where thoughts unaltering alter all the rest?

The grackles gather in the lay-by wood,
and soon the maples will make fists of blood.


## "Blooms All Summer"

Nothing, not even honeysuckle, does.
It's true the rose
may cast up a late blossom, but July
and August's merely prey
to black spot. Plain petunia
is valiant, but come frost
only the sedum, faint on Labor Day,
reddens to rust.

Heal-all, wash-all, weed-all, cool-
or heat-all round the clock:

the formula alike
of industry and of religion.

I go
among the asters now
pinching the dead-heads to prolong the life
a little, winter coming on
and juices draining down.

Living in landscape is to live the poem
re-written and re-written. It is bloom
all summer, if you look at it that way,
old snows recovered in returning May,
et cetera. The advertiser's heart,
like Milton's, lies quite open on the page.
Each year the catalog improves
in gaudy tints and giant promises.

Only the skiers and the skaters cross
the icy hiatus
in flying colors, driven—
but not like ghosts, more like
succeeding petals of some winter garden—
by what deep sortilege,
by what kind art
to trace our seasons on the nursery chart?

## THE BANANA TREE AT CARNEY

Of course your average commuter from up-county
will never notice the banana tree, or if he does
he won't know what it is. It looks as outlandish
as the fake philo in the dentist's office.

I asked the audience what they found obscure
about my work, and one said,
"Words like *sycamore*."
I wouldn't try *paulownia* on him
though they're so common in the Shenandoah
I cropped some pods for Mother, coming home
one Christmas, thinking
how nice they'd look on the mantel, but as usual
with what an adult daughter brings,
my mother said, "What the hell are these things?"

Or, as Disney noted, "What is art
anyway? It's what people like."

I like bananas. I have even been
where they grow, and coffee, jacarandas, tea;
I've been where the sea's
so thick with gannet and with guillemot
they seem familiar as crows at home
in Maryland, where the exotic
confines itself to flame azalea,
snow goose, snow trillium, even sweet gum.

I say the words (oak, apple, ash)
my tongue can cherish, and my fathers sang
(holly and ivy). Now the round atlas
seeds so askew, nobody knows where home was
and I wonder: how does heart
anchor? and in which garden?
what is art?

## Trumpet Vine

Usually they bloom
one blossom at a time
amid a ruddy or an apricot
pod of coming blooms. I keep them
for hummingbirds. I have to cut them back
savagely, or else they'll wreck the fence.
Against some comers, that's the only defense.

Right now (15 July) I spy
my palest one has made a rare bouquet,
like eight flowers flowering in a knot
no plantsman would predict.
It is superb,
a useless, momentary
spot in my window-time.
It will go on
for two days (maybe). Nobody will see.
Nobody ever (least of all the County)
marks Time, much less Beauty. Every year
they mow the lane-edge lilies, and winters
they throw salt on the cedars. When they widened

the Pike, they took
Prosser's azaleas, but they wouldn't pay
a cent, "Improvement,"
they said. When he complained,
they said, "Condemned."

Well, naturally we all stand at the bar
sooner or later, in one avatar
or another. Nature naturing
makes for clean air and overpopulation.
Think what the buffalo would have done
to Kansas, had we left him there.
Think what tarmac has done for Maryland.
The shears are handy. They are in my hand,
and in my ears the ghostly trumpets sound.


ANTHRACNOSE

It makes the leaves
dirty, and then they fall.
A 300-foot-tall
buttonwood is hard to cure.
The lawn in June looks like October.

When we're sick
we know it—that's the hitch.
The chances are
if we cut down the sycamore
the stump would sprout.
Our subtler root
is restless, rings
a planet, chokes
ocean and atmosphere with shoots.
Which shall be whole?
Oh, none since Eden fell, which is to say
time and corruption moved in the first cell
that grew at last a seed in the blind sea
and lifted out man, serpent, fruit, and tree.

We mourn the changes in our scenery
like Adam, who was bored to death
with gardening, but wept
when aphid, mildew, spot,

and scale transformed his garden plot.
He pondered on the fit and the unfit,
but never got the hang of it.

No more do I. I fail
bacillus, virus, and the Japanese
beetle. Also the pearl. As a girl
I loved the microbe hunters.
Later, in medical school,
I learned that disease, like art,
is constant; changes name and shape;
rises and falls
like Appalachians, here and there a peak
called Dante or the Black
Death, called Mozart
or myelitis. Anton Leeuwenhoek,
Lister, Pasteur, Koch,
Paul, Spallanzani, Socrates,
why my old new-world trees?

## Praying in Space

The heart is faster than the eye.
Childhood puts all physics by.
The Muslim spaceman as he may
seeks Mecca in the Milky Way,

feeling how alien a thing
is arm or leg or leaf or wing,
how fragile in the halls of space
the features of the human face;

repeats, as he is bound to do,
among a blond untethered crew,
the scripture of his landless kin
in exile from their origin.

I stand upon my maple lot
and count the blessings I have got;
in love with your creation, Lord,
by summer suspect of your word,

by night beneath the wintry sky,
more willing to put nature by,

and lessoned by the Mussulman
address the space where I began;

neither for profit nor for law,
what Cortez or Columbo saw,
or gentle Mary in her pain,
or Euclid who saw Plato plain,

but for the seven-wondered world,
feature by feature sure revealed,
nature by nature, print by print.
Uncharted Spirit, and unspent,

your errant child, and bound in sense,
I cannot put circumference
to your intelligible sphere,
but seek, like Saud, its center here.

Prayer be my traveller.


# THE WILDERNESS OF THIS WORLD

> Any place in which a person feels stripped of guidance, lost,
> and perplexed may be called a wilderness.
> —Roderick Nash, *Wilderness and the American Mind*

So it might be like
driving in Boston, finding a footpath in
Sussex, doing the income tax.
Or it might be how to deal
with an old stray beagle.

Or it might be like
the dream of the runaway car, your foot
helpless to reach the brake.

Or it might be the fear of death (a place
we're bound to pass)
or of sin, or surgery. One can see
"The Hospital" as a final Kafka plot:
the polyglot
corridor, the gentleman from Peru,
the Okie baby in for a transplant
liver, the principessa, and who knows what
unspeakable labyrinth of tube and chart.

But it is not
the arches (you may thirst) of the Utah desert,
and it is not
(you may hunger) the hooded River of No Return,
Beartooth, Sawtooth, backcountry Yellowstone,
Sinai or Samburu. Out there
good guidance comes by prayer, being the one
possible conversation. You may freeze,
burn, crack, or die,
but somewhere in the clear eternal eye
you are one, not long bewildered, with pronghorn,
lupine and columbine, red rock,
white water, rattlesnake,
and all the fabled folk
of first creation. Lost
perhaps, but overruled,
cleanly delivered back
along the errant track
to promise—not that rancorous hold
of slaughter, of the ram or of the son,
but the one sky
where lamb and lion lie
present in peace, and wilderness
retreats, and paradise
settles our shuffling eyes.

Of course, being domestic
as dogs, who when abandoned
slink to the nearest shack or garbage can,
we should not last a week
in any tent not made by man.
We are not romantic
about blisters and backache. Turning home we cast
a sunset eye up to the last blue ridge
and face, with skins ashine, our heritage.

## Dingman's Falls

*for Tom Foster*

Coming home the wrong way
from Connecticut, save for a glimpse

of the hummocked Hudson and, much farther down
and in, the Lehigh Valley waving grain
at the undulant horizon
(both looking like nothing
so much as American Painting, anonymous,
19th century), is just as many trucks
(but pokier), and less distinguished
townships, acid malls,
Dutch Paradise motels,
and Dingman's Falls.

Being so late
already (dogs on wait
for dinner), I took a side trip
in the Delaware Water Gap,
on Johnny Bee Road, and a twenty-minute walk.
It might have been
(save for park bridges) anonymous American
17th–18th century, or whenever the rhododendrons came
along the stony course, and beech and pine:
a high, thin
silvery water, dropping down
rock ledges in some other Indian
summer.

Once, ramming around
Somerset, I found
East Coker by mistake. There was a plaque
asking our prayers for the repose
of that soul from St. Louis, always a great
jumping-off place. He has them. Tuolumne
has them, and Mt. Anthony, and trees
everywhere. Do not let me hear
the complaints of old ladies. Let me hear
the wisdom of walkers, even when home
is three more hours, and a lifetime burning
in every mirror, especially the odd turning
back, or aside, the moment when we come
original. "Pass on," the flagman says. I do,
convinced of hunger, and the scenic view.

## Duncansby Head

On Duncansby the moors are high,
the winds are higher.
Across the wicked firth toward Hoy
gull and fulmar,
tern and tystie arc and fall,
the lighthouse lambs wag at the teat,
a streaming skylight tatters all
save at my feet
the royal-blooded orchid holds
his alpine inch and will not blow,
though every Pentland skerrie crash
and navies bleach in Scapa Flow.


## Skara Brae

What did they eat?
Cockles and mussels.
What did they sing
in the great stone rings?
"See," the little keeper said,
"three thousand years ago, and they had drains."
Birds' eggs, roots. Whose skins
did they sleep in? Stone knives, stone
bowls (originals in Edinburgh), beads of bone.
"It must have been a storm," he said.
"They left their things."

All too identifiable. The gods
uncovered us again, rolled back the sand
over the sea-bit shelter. A seawall
prevents—how long?—the lobster-loch of Skaill.

"In winter the waves come," he said. And came
like Culain's Hound (our cousin), Julius
Agricola, Thorsten the Red,
over the hearth, the bin, the bed,
the carefully replenished midden.
Nothing but the heart is hidden
that civilization may repeat
(Scapa, Largs, Culloden)
what brought Darius to his feet
and scuttled Eden.

## Duns Scotus's Carinish

They say this rubble "teampull" was your school:
no towers, no branches, acres of poor crofts
alive with lamb and lapwing down to the sea lochs.

And so it must have been then in the long
light of the summer evenings, in the brute
and peaty drear December, in the haar
that shrouded stones still standing long before
Columba fired the machar with his wand,
or Poverty took Francis for a friend.

Nor saint nor subtle doctor I forsook
the systems for a gull upon the wind,
began Atlantic for a grammar book,
and left the crumbling classrooms far behind.


## Tripping

Travel is so much better
in retrospect: no baggage, no Heathrow,
no weather. Oftentimes I think
the world is all behind us, where to choose
Wyoming, or the Zetland voes.

In plain fact it was boredom on the bus,
fellows conspiring how to feed and buy,
too big a sea to skirt the island nest,
cameras and glasses lost.
But these are faded now,
snuffle and sprain, the room without a view.

And bright Balranald fingering the sea
returns with sea pink and bird cry;
or Callanish still standing, forty-seven
thirteen-foot stones accounting Celtic heaven;
Betty saying
of some Lewisian pebble, "This
is the oldest thing you will ever touch." It is all
lapwing and lark. It could be, Dante said,
a single drop of Lethe in the blood,
then ruined Tintern, or the hulk
of Moran shadowing the level lake

rise with an innocence they did not own
here in the kitchen, over the sandwiches,
saying the backward journey still can bless
with half-extinguished beams, as Wordsworth knew:
it is the oldest thing that can touch you.

## Rosa

Twice a year Rosa came
to stay in the back room
where we kept the shoe-clean bench
and the sewing machine.

In those days windows were not uniform,
nor children, tables, beds. A coat from Best
lasted ten years at least, with ups and downs.
I have a summer slipcover—in shreds—
for the old sofa. Nothing new will fit
and nobody'd have skill to alter it.
The last of Rosa's curtains is worn out.

Rosa was tiny, silent, brown, and neat.
She ate in the pantry, which was one step up
from the kitchen, one below
the dining room. Rosa, where did you go
after the Harveys, or the Bartons?
I never learned to sew. I took the old
wrought-iron Singer stands to make a base
for the marble-top. You pedalled that machine
like an organ. I am throwing away
the last of Mother's blouses—store-bought,
naturally, and not my size
but I wore it around the place.

          And soon
there will be nothing, not a stitch
in time to hem us in
percale or calico, velvet or chintz.
Even the hospital linen will be snatched
back, its indelible monogram
new-laundered for newborn
or terminal, whichever we may be
as we aim, threadbare, at the needle's eye.

## Second Childhood

> O wunderliche Zeit, o Zeitverbringen, o Einsamkeit
> —Rilke, "Kindheit"

Once again there is time to spend
in the hammock. When we were children
and books were hard and new, and French, and the piano,
we ripened to some end
unknown, but coming green.

What shall we do? we asked, and sometimes went
for mushrooms, or played cards
on rainy days, collected
starfish, heroes, or made ship models
of balsa wood.

Now it is evening, and the busy street
is silent where we brought
our baskets to be filled
with bread and kindred hours.
We prayed then: May the powers
of table, bed, profession
guard us. We wanted to be good.

But now this odd returning. All is spent
that was expendable; we rest content
with our bargains, what we have become.
We watch the fireflies rising, and wonder, if we were called
inside to supper (though there is no one there
to call us), whether we should go
with so much time to spend.
"Coming," we might shout back, meaning
later, not now.


## Adeste Fideles:
## Christmas, 1982

The bells, if we can hear them, wake
sleeping wounds and joys.
The faithful, if they know it, come
familiar to the crèche,
and Herod's swords are in the street
crowning the prince of peace.

Somalia, El Salvador,
and Lebanon and Eire.
Every mother's face is bent
over an infant's bier,
though he were born and crucified
at Troy or Trafalgar.

Come shepherd, king, and publican,
the narrow year compels
increase, and foison at sea,
and summer in the hills.
What shall we harvest, Nuncio?
What say the bells?

## Christmas, 1984

### 1. The Sons

That bell gone tolling for the heavenly host,
I hear it loud and clear,
and smile to think it settles Plato's ghost
gone wandering many a year,
    and silences the thunder of the grail,
    our April burdens, and our winter's tale.

Long, since those altar apparitions caught
our children's voices up,
or any angel travelled down the light
to hallow what we sought
    at solstice making mantras for the corn
    or beating solemn marches to the tomb.

Ring, bellman, for the ox, the ass, the tree,
the holy rain, the star
that sang like morning in the eastern sky:
all Noah's choir
    gone mumming in our deep and dreamless street
    and one by one turned shadow at the master's gate.

### 2. The Spirit Multitudes

We smile (we must) as sword and spindle mate,
or winking sea and sky,
and every song and sorrow generate
out of a sorcel eye

    that spurned the fox and vixen in the ditch
    and sowed its henges with the dragon's teeth.

And built those halls suspended from a star,
or pyramids on earth,
to house the hosts of Nile and Nineveh
and give them second birth,
    sent off Patroklos with his horse and gear
    and loud Misenus with his idle oar.

The dead do not keep, we know that; do not walk
from some quaint Acheron
into the killing fields that hearken back
to Thebes and Latium,
    but as our hearts and hands and voices move
    to murders or to mercies, so they act and live.

3.    THE FATHERS

I am my father's spit, and oh I chose
my infidelity,
my apple dream, my wide-world wandering house,
my act gone ugly,
    chose in the field, but silently at home
    ponder the measure of the shaman's poem.

Remember making with such memory
as gardens in their seeds
contract, or precipices undersea
drop from their coral heads,
    but sharper, by the sleight of Adam's tongue,
    those tender prospects we were born among.

Remember rounds, and singing in the schools,
and wassail at the fire;
quaint as the soughing of Phoenician sails
to some jet traveller,
    I hear the harp that fashioned Camelot,
    my mummer in the blood that will not let.


# MYSTERIES

Well, now we are old, and everyone admits
over the whiskey that we read
nothing but mysteries. Farewell Flaubert,

farewell Lord Jim and H. C. Earwicker,
and all the venerable crowd
from Moll to Mrs. Ramsay dead.

The Bible, yes, for its sonorities,
the dictionary for its oddments, even trees
or architecture interest—but not much:
as Uncle William mentioned, we are out of touch.

Means, motive, opportunity: the grisly form
repeats itself in endless variation,
solved once, and ever to be solved again—
the telltale print, the bent twig in the garden.
We dreamed of love and mercy in our youth.
Now morning hastens, and we study truth.


## Video Games

In Claude Lorrain, the trees win every time.
The violent spots of color are a game.
The dragon's blood, the swordplay on the shore,
the embarkation of the fleet across the silent water,
all dwarfed, dwarfed Helen, Io, Aeneas,
the Holy Family stopping on a grass
that never was in Sinai. Peasants dance
and satyrs pipe, their tiny stories all
leafy, and all
escaped the stony street and hovering temple.

So these, avoiding schoolwork, play
at whoops and rockets on a screen
uncluttered by both stone and green
parameters. Giant Mars
fragmented into points of light
consumes himself in deserts of the night.
Here happy bloodless families hone their skills:
Sue's ship's in bits, and Bill has all the castles.
But Brother Dragon wings the upper air
weightless in orbit as the angels are
and free as Lucifer to strike his earth.
Space-fox! Sue yawns into her Coke,
and Sally's boyfriend, bored, begins to stroke
Sally, but Bill is dead set now to win.
Dad, blasted, ambles toward another gin

at slipper-speed. Mom grumbles. Newton gapes,
and Freud erases "Father" from his tapes.

Claude's careless creatures (here St. Joseph reads
old tales, in respite between pines and palms;
Jason, Odysseus, Paris hoist their sails;
the local Venus flees the local arms)
in studio-apprentice postures, all
picnic, or prepare to fall. Who cares?
The sun, magnificently absent, stares,
apex of every scene,
cloudless, clairvoyant, and Copernican.

I exit from the beltway, overviewed
by Channel 13's copter, where right lane
must turn right—you miss it,
proceed at once to the shock-trauma unit.
I unwind down the lane, lay off
my greaves and groceries, take the dogs a walk
into the poor three-times-cut-over woodlot.
There's slow-grow beech, maybe twelve inches thick
already, an occasional oak
and tulip poplar. They will never shelter,
as once, red Conewago, briefly daubed
into the picture. Here's the crossing-rock,
the mountain of its island continent.

                        Late secret light,
the wine of day that nourished Milton, bent
upon his darkling canvas, far from Rome,
lays on the ferns that gentle elder-root
its mysteries. Pebbles play
the water music as I wander home.
Last raven sounds his Indian Alert.
A vesper sparrow calls Convert, Convert!


## HOMAGE TO COROT

Vermeer could paint the light, Rembrandt the dark,
Whistler the fog, and several the flesh,
the fur (though mostly workshop), and the face
(as Velasquez), occasion, race
(as Delacroix), the endless
varieties of fruit and forest. Go

to the Hermitage. There
they stack them layer on layer,
dead rabbits and dead fish. Only Corot
could paint the air.

So said Andrew Marbot, suicide
at thirty (we presume,
the corpus being vanished into thin
air, near Urbino,
out on a ride). We vanish all,
hare and hill-town, martyr and general,
brutal Courbet, smooth Raphael,
and (sharper than a serpent's tooth) Clouet.
The difference is their record of the way
we took the air, horse,
rider, rooftop, sail,
jewelled contessa—all that list
long as the living eye that fixed them there
breathless in air.


## Notes from Cézanne

Cannot find model. Tablecloth will do
in a pinch, but bedspread better, having blue
border. Will Mme. Brémond miss
her saints? It is too far
to the mountain. Quarry time.
Force beauty. Force the eye. We do not see
by roof and pasture, street,
pipes in their faces, shuffle hands at cards.
Hand traces
subtler arrangements, balances of pears,
brushstrokes on gravity. Lost heroic towers,
Olympian dreams, what were they but a knot
to stay the soul in flight?
Apples will do as well as Sheba's cloak
to say how nature is a trick of light,
and under or behind or at the very
point, pivot of cone or cylinder or sphere—
but nothing will stay still. My apples riot
like wrestlers. I have tamed
no muscle, not the burning eye

that brands this tinder table . . . They will call
it "still life." As they wish—
rock, snowfall, ginger jar, the artist's face.


## Arias

### Che faro
What do you do
without Eurydice? Your work.
A-stumble in the dark
hallow-rid middens
who would not look back?

Lost foot, forward foot . . .
the dust behind that makes the music float
in air, in airs.

For Orpheus' lute
we have no ears but ghostly. He is gone,
savaged, bestrewed.
We walk in dust and blood.
Looking behind, we make his music good.

### Ecco ridente
Day stops upon her rising. Can you believe
you were once so young that time
went radiant or set
by your pulses? That you were,
in fact, an opera star, though now you go
checking each hour at the shop, occasionally
humming some light air, or (rarely)
rising to watch the dawn come up,
certain that time (it will not) will never stop?

### Deh Vieni
This, the heart's
and not the limbs' commitment,
is our best moment. Limbs rebel,
wander, decay. You do not need to know
that yet, although you have seen it.
Keep your feet in the garden,
Susanna. Bid him come.
There need be no expulsion.

CASTA DIVA
The lily, the lily, the rose I lay.
I have made offering,
ablution, vow.
There is no way.
I am the fool, the fool in the play.
Would I have it differently? Ah shades
lamenting, welcome me, and we will sing
how love is king.

O ISIS UND OSIRIS
Whoever you are, gods, I am praying
not for the joint but for the disparate pair.
For us, the separation is harder
than the coming together. We asked neither.
You have taught us passion, taught us sacrifice
(but never on your part). Teach us how to fare
in the suddenly empty air.

DOVE SONO
Where are the pony moments
and the skating?
You wake up only once.
That's the day after the prince
has come and gone. He'll be there in the flesh,
drinking his orange juice, but far away
where you aren't sleeping, Beauty.
Then you sing.
Then nights are tenderer, remembering.

DI PROVENZA
From the day you leave home
on your own two feet, you can never drown
two musics. Loud adventure
avails not; failure
avails not. A certain light
on a street, on a tree; the kitchen light; the mountain:
what bred me, what I am.

AI NOSTRI MONTI
There in our hills we sang.
I hear them calling
in this cold courtyard. It is time to go.
Firelight, moonlight, banjo, dulcimer.
We shall be again as we were.

## Translation

"There is no translation of this piece. It's about
a mountain and a lake." Thus the PBS
commentator on the Sunday concert.
It was something Finnish.

One: there is no translation
of lakes and mountains, not without program notes,
which is what we are missing, hearing over the air
some waves that might suggest to us fire or water,
might remind us of calm or storm,
or tell us: remember to move the hose
and take in the laundry.
Or they might say
tomorrow is Marion's birthday.

Two: the lake and the mountains will do
as well as anything. The mere suggestion
conjures Whiteface and Winnisquam
and all things Appalachian. Equally well,
it conjures Buttermere and Furness Fell.
But not Naivasha. It's a bracken hill,
snowy in season; pine is sentinel. The level
lake may ship a hero or a gull;
flamingos would be fanciful.

Or three: it might be blood, not water. It might be
most intimate pulsation; breath not wind;
not shadows on the rock, but on the mind;
synapse, not Indian Leap; muscle not stone,
not leaf, not bole, but marrow bone.

And four, it is a new
creature, very like
the folk of Lyell's or of Darwin's book,
survivor's fruit
of quake and cataclysm, glacial sheet
and rich organic soup—no more than I
an imitation reality.

And five, but it is not alive
except I read it. It is pen and ink.
It is a world, René, because I think.
The Bishop went one better: who thinks me
that thinks the crackle of the falling tree

is soundless if there's nobody about
the forest? George did not think that. His ear
was keener. He could hear
ghosts in the garden, and they sang, "I am
Plato and Piney Mountain, Kinneret
and Prospero, Katahdin and Mozart."
He heard them sing. He made his own
translation.

## Silence

I read of a traveller who in Ladakh
received the mountains' gift:
silence. He called it (although British)
a Buddhist silence.

At home in cricket August
night is louder than day, or say
the voices of the dumb—
creek and tobacco bloom—
make closer music.

No man,
mariner or Indian,
has not received a silence, praised
that silence with a name,
whatever's handy: Zeus,
or Zoroaster, or Jesus. Some praise
is closer: Stony Face,
Star-maiden, Hungry Bear.

I do the same
as travellers in Kashmir—
name it because it is there.

## Subtracted Memories

*on a poem by John Ashbery*

Scratch nine out of ten American
poets and you get
watery Wordsworth, watery Thoreau.

Even you, you mention the smell
of blossoming privet. We don't
have privet anymore. It used to hide
the clothesline from the garden, maybe eleven,
twelve feet high, and how well
I remember the shearing, lest it grow too tall
to reach from the next-to-last step
of the old wooden ladder. "Cut *in,* cut *in,*"
called my mother. "It needs light
at the bottom." I hadn't
thought of it for years, might never have done,
and this just one
of the prunings trundled to the Ridgelys' pit
of bottomless decay—I suppose it
may have been a root cellar. And the poet,
rooting around, restores the senseless leaves
and clippings that were never history,
die daily, and will never die,
only repeat, like waves that are
always the same water, although we
do not believe it.

## Assorted Masters Perform

They look like gentlemen, and speak
like gentlemen. Rather much to the surprise
of the lay audience, they wear ties.
They speak of mothers, fathers, daughters, wives,
the trees, the animals, the whales, the stars.
(They are all creationists, being our seniors
and having been there.) Sober on the stage
they update, verse by verse, our youth and age.

The unselfconsciousness is careful. Too,
the anecdote, the well-rehearsed bon mot
to hide the embarrassment of being here
behind the mike, light-blinded to the crowd.

"I see," my friend said, driving home
past the Kennedy Center, "what is wrong with my brother.
He keeps it all inside." Oh blessed art
that lets us put between ourselves and that
kingdom of chaos where we all began
a stance, a speech, a scrim.

## For the Keeper of MSS

Earth was the first book, and the first pen
a stick or stone. Then color—was it blood
or mulberries? And then the medium
improved: papyrus, vellum.
How much the others aided our illumination.
Even yet
if not the quill, we dip
the bristle into vegetable dyes
and write the world before our eyes.

You have to scrape
the hair off, patiently,
for parchment, peel the eye,
too, to make sense of Noah's zoo,
or John's six-winged angel (and with twain
he flew). Or was it some other
evangelist, enisled in gold and blue
upon a page in some gray northern room
with ox and eagle, lion and man,
to cheer brocaded ladies at their hours
who had that vision?

Our eyes have histories
or how else should we look
upon Aeneas' or Iskander's book,
or spy upon the great
and gilded prospect of our first estate?
For all here's garden, where we fell
from fatal notice of the speaking tree,
and everywhere are flowers brilliantly
climbing the margins of our works and days;
even death and hell,
embowered in the codex and the scroll,
open our hearts like April promises.

And if such flowers on earth were never seen,
some keeper of the leaves has kept them ever green.

## Recipes

When, late from France, I introduced
quiches to the campus, they became so common
I felt compelled to change my specialty.
It couldn't be cassoulet; you couldn't get
the Toulouse sausages. It couldn't be langoustines.
How often I wish
Americans could learn to grow crawfish.

Of course I gave my recipes away.
Last night I gave Esterlee
the zucchini casserole, and she'll give it to Jessie,
and so it goes. No keeping a secret. I may revert
to Maryland chicken and angel cake. The fit survive,
and the raw materials
don't change much in a lifetime, but they change:
there was no tea at Stonehenge. It's hard to think back—
no beans, no wheat—
but somehow there was always something to eat.
So much is fixed, but how it's mixed
with foreign influence, like wars,
weather, and trade winds, genes
and genius, who's to tell?
I poach the flounder in my mother's dish.
The scholars say my mother was a fish.
The strict constructionists say man
strutted on two legs of his own
all around Eden. Maybe he did,
sharing his recipe with only God, and his spare rib
with woman.

She found apples
good eating. Naturally she shared.
She discovered blood,
guts, seasonings; how to make stock; how best to grow
salads and sesames; and how to raise
bread. One son discovered how to raise the dead
but he never told.

Now she grows old, beyond experiment.
The harvests shrivel; hands are obsolete
in the modern kitchen, simples in the sickroom.
Her travelling grandchildren have much to learn
in secret space, where the bright planets turn
ocean, perhaps, come shore, come kitchen garden.

## The Economy, the Environment, etc.

On Islay the distillers
are fighting the goose-fanciers
(Greenland white-fronted) for the peat:
to cut or not to cut. In Wales
the locals gather at Llanwrtyd Wells, to "Halt the Curse
of the Conifer." Here at home
we are trying to save the serpentine
barren at Soldier's Delight from the County's so-called
Growth Management Plan.

And yet it would be a strange world without birds,
spruce, whales, like living on oil rigs, or carrying your air
in with you, as you have to do
in water or the Johns
Hopkins library; strange
words like Bunnahabhainn, Nant-y-brain,
Wyoming, soon
to our successors hardly known,
possibly saved in some Smithsonian
keep, to be cracked
like Linear B or Cro-Magnon. Stranger to see
ourselves; like leaves, becoming history,
peat, coal, plastic resource
of comers like Mars, or eohippus.


## I Love New York, Virginia, Channel 2, Pier 1, etc.

My parents taught me what to love.
We often disagreed. Mother re-read
*The Good Earth;* I read *The Wings of the Dove.*
She liked Victor Herbert,
and I liked Schubert. Well, no snobbish matter;
we agreed in principle
except about girdles and make-up.

Dad thought ballet
was silly, but he went with me
and counted tours jetés
out loud in the Lyric. He was a sailor,
shanghaied by Procter and Gamble.
I get seasick

but I like canoes, and some day yet
I'll do the Boundary Waters.
So much for daughters.

I don't like bumper stickers
proclaiming Jesus, or the Orioles. Virginia is
for lovers of Virginia born and bred. The adopted
never master the vowels. True love
is not puffed up, and advertiseth not; cannot be bought
or sold; is seldom caught in script.
How do I love thee? Who knows how?
or why Yeats stopped at the ninth bean row,
or why I am sick at heart
to think that when we meet,
these days, no sweet
bird sings. And sicker yet
to think of those I cannot meet.

Where they stop, listen, look—
there's no train there, no ticket, no discount,
no reservation, and no cheers
for the home team. It could be
the vacation bargain of your life.
Everything's free, and you could make it look
like Culpepper, or Grundy—even New York.

## Cooking the Heart

Look, any cook
has got to be good at guts,
and I don't mind
gizzards and backs. But some
parts boggle me, especially hearts.

What is the quaint
anatomy whereby the saint
is reliqued, tibia
or tooth or fingerbone,
or any odd apparel that we own?
Say, bridal veil,
shroud, infant tress, toenail,
feather, or face—whatever is the fashion,
we die and pass it on.

Into the legend, into the stock:
Adam, Veronica, Cecilia, Paul,
Aquinas, Clare, and here
a chicken for the pot
with parsley, bay leaf, celery, and carrot,
liver and lights. The tiny heart—
is this the mighty seat
of gallinaceous passion? Ah, that's it,
our skewed mythology, as if a piece
of muscle pumped our art.

I can't divide it. Why do I always feed it
to Max, my favorite
terrier? Why does he
regard it as a special delicacy?

So much for savage customs, mystery,
Romantics, Catholics, and Valentines.
I fish the heart out on the tines
of Mother's broken-handled fork
for Max, who jumps.
He's been near twice a decade at the pumps.
I stir the stew with metaphoric finger.
It wants more salt, and half an hour longer.

Dear hearts, whose recipes I follow
(though not religiously), I've plucked, skinned, scaled,
even dissected in my time.
One ought, I guess, to harden. But instead
at 60 I grow simpler in the head,
open the screen to let out the stray moth
and swallow gallons of synthetic broth.
And yet for all our chemistry, because
of all our chemistry, we prey,
sanctioned by Genesis, god-fearing Darwin,
necessity, and southern living.

                            Hen,
some of your relatives would pick me clean,
had they the chance. Ours is an odd communion,
but not heartless.
We raise each other, blood- and bodiless.

# A Dream of Reunion

I am always going a journey; I am always missing the boat.
They are with me at the outset; they are also the ones
I am going to meet, those first not-I
faces. I stop them at eleven,
maybe fourteen, though we were five or six
in kindergarten, and we fix
our smiles at sixty, at reunion,
having little in common.
This solves the problem, who the people were
Cain and his siblings married, for the school was there
all along, just waiting
for our expulsion. I pushed my brother
into the radiator. I thought the world
of Mrs. Levring and Mrs. Naylor.

In this particular dream, before the procession,
we primped in the senior room, in our long dresses.
The piano started to boom
the march from *Aida*. I'd mislaid my comb.
I said, "I'll meet you at the study-hall
door," but I never did.
It was a series of near misses.
I ducked around the old gym, took the bus
to the corner, where it skidded on the ice. I went into a barn
to ask directions, but they stole
my wallet, and a bull
slobbered all over my dress.
I walked past Mother beckoning at the gate.
I could hear the music, then the prayer: "Watch over
our school, O Lord, as its years increase, and bless
and guide thy children . . . keeping them ever
unspotted from the world." Dishevelled and too late
I hitched a ride to the mountains. Oddly enough,
I was expected, though the shoddy guesthouse
was full of strangers.
I never did graduate.

And now I wonder if I wanted to.
Our uniforms were blue
cotton; only Anne Byrd
wore wool in winter. I did pass,
in fact, but missed the ceremony
due to the quinsy; went a separate track. I seldom heard

from any of them. We sing
the old song at Centennial: "Come
let us gather . . ." Is it possible
after the long division that we learned
together, after the maps
of yellow rivers, the long ships
off Sunium, the bloody Pax
Romana that we traced
roadways into the provinces
to Boudicca, to Vercingetorix?
We marched in step
like legions under Roman-numeralled
banners, off into History
ourselves. Mother threw out
my Euclid when I married and they moved
to town, pure reason
proving irrelevant to all but children.

Yet what is it that speaks
in my dream but some straight line to the one
center of these excursions, one alive
in every part? We bravely sing (though I've
forgotten the last verse) to every class
that has been or will be. *Ex sole
ad solem.* I do not forget
my trying-to-be-English garden. Home
would not be home without it. Like some
antediluvian Darwin at bird tracks
and wallows, under Uluru, the rocks,
my dream-tongue speaks.

Else why, among so many and more dear,
do your beginning faces gather where
I am going, over the mountains, Eve
a-wander, big with promise, looking in
to taxing shelters, the polluted air
of stables, the exploded star—
Polly and Helen, Betty and Eleanor?

## Touchstones II

How easily the firm
foundations rise, at the corners

of day—awake, abide—
and seasons—hail
and hearken. Ear and tongue
ancestral guard the graves
they move among.
At the hours
we are most with ourselves (as gardening
or playing the piano) we revert
of a sudden from Joplin, or even Bach,
to Duke Street. Neither Mary nor Ruth
will know what I am talking about.
Philip will look it up. Gwalchmai,
Melita. Bill
might remember from the Easy Tunes
for Beginning Recorder. Geneva. Gaudeamus
pariter.

And at the hour
of death, or of our operation, the camp hymn
will come to us, that used to be
#120, Dear Lord
and Father of Mankind. But it is Mother
we will be thinking of then, and wishing
her near, all love,
divine, excelling. We will be thinking
of our past selves, the camper, and the cox
who lost the race. And Miss Dalton telling us
that was no disgrace. Rise up,
fight the good fight, fling out
the banner, let it float.

Lost hearts, lost hands, lost voices. Shore to shore
the airwaves clack and croon, imperilling all
whom solemn silence at the peak of night
might once have signalled, as on Horeb height
the fire broke from him, pitching sun and star.

Old Holyface, and fairest lord, forgive
our foolish memories and fluent ways,
the water where we walk, our triune years,
our storm shelters: old Winchester, and new
Sarum, we sing, weeding the drive, or rooting
the burdocks out around the cellar door,
Watchman, St. Hilda, Veni Creator.

## Moving in Memory

1
Moving within memory, I can count
Virginia, Maine, Vermont,
and to a wild extent
Wyoming. I am sick
of my blasted county: Albert Lacey's truck
ten times a day; beltway; industrial park; high density
housing; and Hartline's oak
sickened, that might have seen
Calvert's lieutenants dickering with red men.

There is a nice old house for sale
in the city. There is always a house for sale
in the city, but the price is steep. I should weep
to leave my star magnolia, peonies,
and dogwood. Should I relocate? Why not
Paris, London, Rome,
Shropshire, or the Dordogne? Some ancient dam
lies dusty among them,
but not my seasoned tongue. Just here
Grandfather cries from quaint Annapolis, near where
great-uncle Burton found
the clovis point, only two of that kind
ever, the other
near Chesconnessex. Here the bones
cry up, "Forsake us not." The roads,
however bent, are Joppa still,
Merryman's, Mantua, Paper Mill, and all
my eyes have known them, known
the quarry trail down the Loch Raven
peninsula, the twelve-year track to school,
the boxwood Mother brought up from Eyre Hall.

2
But think of pilgrims—Swedes
in South Dakota, secret Chinamen
in Manitoba, in the night
opening a childish book
that spelled Adventure, or Escape.
They were not all young
(Father Anchises, Father Abraham).
Some mothers never mastered the new tongue.
Some spoke of seas to unbelieving children.

Each, in a secret space,
put on his childish face
(how many faces strong)
of Uzhgorod, Cosenza, Aberdeen.

3

Descartes, you were fortunate to have had
no need of France, no nature to depend
on anything material—so you said. And wouldn't we all
like to believe you? But even before the Fall
fixed us in time articulate
(cousin and calendar, hearth and helpmeet),
our eyes opened on light:
rift valley, tarn, fin, feather, fur, and fruit.

If you'd been born in Cody, say,
you'd think, but you'd think differently,
and if you'd been born
no place (which is a contradiction
in terms)—say, issued straight
from the Thinker into this air—
what would you think about?
Your thought would be (precious presumption)
his thought, which may be with us, or may not.
In any case we're only sharecrop
hands and sandy feet. The spirit
moves within memory, and only there. And whither
it may be winged (or not), it words its prayer
"sun," "wilderness," "wind," "breath," and "daily bread,"
"neighbor," and "trespass." We are set
contextual. Lest, brother, we forget.

4

There is of course Achilles, Moses, Ur,
dodo and dinosaur,
with spiny evidence of being there,
as I have been
carrelled awhile in red-barn Bennington,
or picking fossils on the Goosewing Trail,
or looking forward to the foreign mail—
F. is in Egypt, E. in Israel.
We travel all. My trespassed realm of green
takes sometimes Arden's shade, or Paestum's sheen.
My life takes light from where the light has fallen,
darkling I dream, and dream of Eden garden.

How do you dream, René, how body out
pure loveless thought?

5
In words, no doubt, those words
coaxed from our cradle in some foreign tree. We see
by leaflight, and we name the leaf
rock maple, sassafras,
laurel, or blue-eyed grass.
World be my rock.
In unimaginable eternal night,
where no sun shines, if light
breaks on the purblind spirit
gently—and such a light
that some have called it music—how translate
at Lethe, these rank waters of the heart, how tide us over
alive to stranger parts
than ever Gabriel with his country speech
coasted, in love of the world's wish?

I word this in the memory,
Dylan, of your gull-sided grave
and winged words across the spit of Wales;
of Roman nightingales
sickening for Hampstead; of our Greek
sisters that cry
old nursery tales from Daulis, dipping by
their dobe nests low over
polluted Long Green Creek.
How, in another world, shall Adam speak?

6
So it all adds up: "a vernal wood,"
"the land of spices," "something understood."
Air breathes me, fire warms, fair weather slakes,
earth makes, unmakes;
makes in us most where blooms of the same tree
(dogwood, chokecherry)
come bid to care, and move in memory.

## A Valediction

In the great shade of August, under the sycamores,
if it is hard to imagine Piedmont without trees,
think of Sahara, or the Hebrides.

Yet they are coming down,
the German woods, and templed Oregon;
deep in the Gros Ventre, and the Amazon,
the chain-saws buzz like locusts all day long.

Where did pollution enter: acid rain,
base power? Caryatids cannot keep;
the Law and Prophets smoulder on the heap
like California. We are left
whatever tinder memory can heft.
The very stuff of cells
forgets the fire, the glacier, the sea-swells,
sweet-breathing air, and finally ripe earth.
Nature and Liberty uphold a weight
like chastity—too grave, too great.

So poets enter, and forbid to mourn,
since by division we grew
into ourselves, and growing die,
still wanting our reunion
with earth or sea or sky. What planetary dust
made Cain the first contender for our meat,
saw Babylon and Rome fall out,
saw Donatello and Mozart? saw trees?
I shy at purposes,
and shrivelling, like the branch of Noah's dove,
praise passengers like leaves of love.

# New Poems

## Keeping Time

We are all clock-children, sugarbush and bear,
the swallows gathering now, the nebulae,
though different times are set
plantain and planet.

Like us, the sun asleep
lights up the underworld.
But that is childish talk
from Dante. But for him
they would not be in time,
those antic faces, drawn
from history to dream.

Out in the compost heap
the severed gardens yield
food for the future crop.

And are there dials set
for violence that cuts short—
those battles in the mist,
that dagger in the breast?
What dire alarm
delivered Absalom
to Joab in the wood,
or Caesar to his blood?

Is there a second clock
for conscience? Glaciers crack;
the inarticulate
creatures decline—the dinosaur, the crane.
They do not read
our time-pieces; they do not make
our moan; they do not sin,
so cannot ask our question: sleepers wake?

The summoned sun goes down
on white Old Bennington
this late September dusk.
Our granite obelisk
tells revolution too. And there they lie,
hero and Hessian,
in maple elegance
for tourist shot and shoe.

"And who was Robert Frost?"
"Some kind of writer," says
the knowledgeable one.

And Andrew Marvell dust,
who made time run.
And old Methuselah,
who took it slow.

## Storm King

What I think is
he was brought in on the storm.
That early season, all the trees bowed down
in their leaves.
There was no room at the inn, and no power
at home. Everything stopped.
The food spoiled in our freezers.
Young men with saws and rope
made a mint clearing up.
We were all desperate,
could not do laundry, had the children
all day, said good-bye
to the asters and the phlox.

      Big zebrabacks
are not unknown here, although Tom says
they're very rare, the flushed fawn
belly and the scarlet crown. "Beneficial,"
says Audubon, and "very common
in the southeast." But life
surprises us with sightings. At the post office
the summerfolk will say, "Did you see the double rainbow?"
Or, "We didn't know
you had coyotes."

Still to move
with nature, still to praise
shy flocks, the poet's paradise
and hunter's plenty . . .

      So, my guest,
lone red-belly, I did my best
with nuts and suet for twelve days
before you took Egyptian ways.

## Jan. 1, 1991

When prayer could change the weather, or a tree
be holy, then we knew
who we were, where we lived
in the middle kingdom.
If we moved we carried,
to found the new house,
tent-pole, totem, cross,
the *lares* and *penates*, those who blessed
our little space.

When the great rock
of winter cracked,
the ghost greened with the crop,
befurred, befeathered, and confessed.

But now the man
of infinite horizons monitors
the clear-cut stars;
and for how few,
now we have changed the weathers,
is the bare new year new.


## September 1, 1990

How does the sky know
how we season here? The first clear air
for months, no fleck in the blue,
and overnight it is fall—
milkweed and jewel-weed and morning sweater.

Do maples feel their changes? Should we pray
to drop in autumn glory?
A very sympathetic fallacy, impervious
to science, for we still
people the all-night planets, who have trod
the barren moon, and set a signal stone
in the Cathedral window, for Grade 4
to gape at—it's their favorite scripture.

Artemis of the changes, you
astonish still such ancient eyes
as greet September with a Greek surmise.

# A Book

Dusting the top shelf, containing
Gawain to Vaughan, and including
two complete Spensers (paper), stuck behind,
I found F.Q., Bk. 1, a stubby faded red
buckram edition. Why
I've kept it, I don't know. The flyleaf goes:
E. Harding, 118
Commonwealth, March 17,
1885. Ros. Randall, B.M.S.,
Clare Beirne, and Randall, J.,
IV A.

No one will add
to this family saga, conjuring up
more readily than the Complete,
Una, Duessa, the Spenserian stanza
we had to write for Branham. Mine
had a doe and a virgin, properly
for a twelve-and-a-half-year-old
in that day, *illo tempore*. Where will it go,
this underlined and over-noted, slow
and stately text? "A simile
is *like* or *as*"—this in my grandmother's
elegant penmanship. Then Aunt Rosamond's
marginal "Speranza = Hope."
Cousin Clare's pencil, on end-papers: "Class
should not always have same Pres., and Bryn Mawr does!"
Mine, I'm afraid, says, "Wolcott
can you come over Sat?"

Think of the cantos taking faithful shape.
Clarendon's ed., the Dean of Durham, states,
"The life of Spenser had few incidents
and little certainty." He entertained
Raleigh, W.; Sidney, P. He knew the Queen.
He saw Kilcolman and his baby burn. "And so his life
withered away." What withering.

I need shelf-room. I could abandon
this relic, but I put it down
dusted, behind the Malory. To K. and J.
Randall, I (Fidelia?) might say:
"Arthur is coming. Pass it on."

## Hamlet

The places you have to pass
are ignorance and bliss.

How do we honor our mothers
after our finished fathers?
Achilles set to die,
Ulysses in a pig's sty . . .

I should have been a gentleman
of peace—a house,
a library, the hounds.
How came I out of bounds?
Like Adam, by a voice.

Lancelot wept, went holy, lived to tell
his brave beads his betrayal.

Consign me to the angels, friend,
that I may wind
through naked worms, and naked come
into a clean kingdom.


## Bedivere's Tale

I am Bedivere, dying. My story is this.
An ordinary knight, not much educated,
fairly good at missions. The Archbishop
wanted to send me to Rome, but I'm not a religious,
more like a refugee.
My eyes go west. I hope
someone will mind the garden, now I must
cast it away. I took good care of it.
Remember to bell the cat. I hear the birds
now: take me, take me, take me. Away, away, away
across the wide Missouri.

It was nothing. I always see water. My old eyes . . .
So you want to hear it again? It was a dream,
I tell you. An old dream of Come Again
(they said that in the trenches, did you know?
"Arthur is coming—pass it on").
I should have married. But my love went out
on that lake. It was not

as they say. I am not, as they say,
holy. Mad, maybe—
that we never know. Percival, Tristram, yes,
but gladly mad. And Galahad
making a film all his life, our white-haired boy.

Nor am I a thief. Lord, what a filthy lie.
And from them who hardly left the bloody linen
on all that field, and still go picking bones.
There's Gawain's skull at Dover, and Lord knows
where else. Only Lucan
I buried at dawn, where he had fallen
at the King's feet, and where the dream began.
And I kept nothing, sword nor seal nor ring,
but crossed the forehead of my mother's son
and stumbled here to meet another death,
Arthur—and where then was Excalibur?

It is true I disobeyed. Nor did I think
he wandered in his mind. But he was helpless
to move, of Mordred's stroke, and more . . .
he must have gone, even without the wounds.
What were an Arthur, mewling at a shrine?
And what were a new Table, a new town?
Love in one lifetime satisfies a man.
Each of us has one mother, and one king.

And this I knew obscurely on that night
I took the brand. How marvellously light
it was, and here a scabbard stone
worn by his mail. I put my fingers round
the hilt he'd grappled more than any hand,
even hers.
It didn't fit me, but I liked to touch
there where the lion's sinews made the lip
good. I ask you, have you had
a mother, brother, sister of your blood,
a lady, or a prince—Lord, even a dog—
you would not have remembered by some
object: a chain—she wore that—or a cross,
a book leaved over, linen, or a lace?
It is to touch the dead—that's what I thought
the second time. I didn't even look
at it. Perhaps he understood,
but kept his purpose, with my body's aid.

The last time and the worst time, though resolved
to do his bidding and deliver whole
the weapon to the waters where the moon
made dark lap over light, there I drew out
the great blade from the sheath and read
what none but he had read, and what has been
these twenty years the object of my thought,
my love of him, my relic, and my hope.
"Take me," it said on one side, and reversed
"Cast me away." I gathered and I cast.

He arched, stood upright, plummeted. The lake
closed, and the lappings moved dark-bright, dark-bright,
seamless as if you slipped your arm to pluck
a pebble. But there was no arm, I say.
Samite is laureate's language, like six wings
is laureate's language, so that we may see,
as next I saw, bearing my heavy liege,
the lake become a sea, the hills sink down,
and all that water open toward the moon.

The barque? Yes—but remember dreams in snow,
and dreams in drowning. I had been awake
for two days running. Yes, I saw it come,
silent, in pantomime, but not of mourning.
Three figures of the old school, draped, untelling
gender, or provenance, or destination.
They took him, laid him down, and turned their faces
westward, across the sea. The moon went down.
When I awoke it was the birdless tarn
you know, where diving boys if they dared
might look among the leeches for that brand
forever, or the shape of Merlin's child,
the sea-born. For the bones of Uther's son,
they lie here in the chapel where he came
that night, or morning, of my only dream.

## BEDIVERE'S RHYMES

1
With Merlin shut in rock
the ancient tables shook.
No man walked on water

or bred a holy book
but had a serpent father
who sang him to the lake
where the great sword was brandished,
the hilt thrust
into his hand of dust
to blood his little earth
the single length of breath.

2

Standing in Orkney's circled stone
I saw a ship sail round the moon.
I saw translated Galahad
follow Sangreal, where it led.

I saw at stony Camelot
the Table fashioned by our sweat
and bloody stroke and sentence sharp.
"But no," said Merlin, "by a harp."

I saw a king laid lifeless out,
another ferried in a boat
to Avalon. At last I write
as blessed by blindness as by sight,

like Milton, who abandoned us—
the native rain, the native rose—
to wage his battle in the skies
and build bedevilled Paradise.

Imagination in the tree
pointed our pathways to the sky,
and Adam on his feet of clay
went his appointed way.

That power in the serpent's mouth,
that angel's presence in the dawn,
that promise as I come to death,
that sword, that stone.

3

The lake is never silent, the sword is never still.
The word and wound
from Scapa Flow to Narragansett Sound
wash, warn, and kill.
Leaves on the maple in December light
I see, and see the leafless moon,

man-trod land of stone, more strange
than passing henge to stony henge
along the Roman's road.

Lancelot through Amesbury wood
rode weeping for his love,
and heard the ancient monoliths
his great sins reprove,
and dwelt among us holy,
and heard the angels come.
Fifteen hard days that body
we carried to the tomb.

What sleeps at Glastonbury, Brogar, or Joyous Gard?
Bones in their ruined pride,
or swordless spirits fled
wherever Hector went
degraded in his mail?
Do the three ladies sit
nursing Sangreal?
And are we equal come,
Elaine and Guinevere,
Judas Iscariot, and Oedipus the seer
who could not see himself?
Again the voices came
through olive and through laurel
to sing the homeless home.

4
I made these rhymes from Memory, bound,
Imagination free.
Two sisters of the spinning ground
are both alike to me.
I dream the third.

As it has been and still will be
under the moon or cross:
no way we can tell our gain,
our loss.

And no way we can tell our word
who wander in the mist
by sad division and sword,
by Morgan kissed,
by Merlin prisoned in the tree,
by music blessed.

## Heimweh

Schubert, I know your lieder
by heart, although I do not play
and seldom read the text.
It is not necessary.

Many thousand strong,
by Isar and by Seine,
Afton or Chesapeake,
we long.

So when I say,
"dogwood," or, "Long Green Creek,"
or even, "poison ivy," turned so fiery in the fall,
here on a starker hill gone wandering,
I only speak. You sing.


## Nearly Anon.

"Nothing is known," it says here of some Renaissance composer.
So much the better. Did he wear glasses?
do back exercises? was adulterous? gay?
behind in his taxes? a soldier (unlikely),
a lay brother (maybe), a sycophant at court or altar?

We know, from his *Fantasia*, he had talent, know he knew
how breath and gut can conjure miracle
at work, how in our dark environs we repeat
that first enlightening act, to make
music of time—the day, the night, the first tree
in the midst of the garden, which we nearly ate.


## Hey Baxter

*for Clare and Nat*

The playground is as noisy
as a confabulation of crows. They call,
"Hey Baxter," and, "Hey Beth." They climb
tire pyramids, they swing,
they sway on the quaking bridge.

The School Board tells us every year
they are our heritage.

If "youth is wasted on the young"
(meaning they don't like
Coquilles St. Jacques or artichokes,
or don't direct
their energy to weeding, or their attention
to Sunday school—I hear the Baptists
calling them in),
I don't agree.

They teach us weary
drudges to believe, at desk or pan,
how things began
foot-forward, from the swing
to the deck, from the deck to the tower.

Hey Baxter.


## Twenty-One Turkeys

*for Short and David*

Twenty-one turkeys
amaze our eyes, come travelling
north from the Berkshire Museum (Art
and Natural History). It says there boa constrictors
do not harm humans. False Laocoön!
not to mention Eden.

               On Route 7
nobody stops, but if they had a gun
(or a camera in Yellowstone)
they'd stop to shoot the hideous buffalo.
Turkeys are ugly too. We have waited
twenty years to see one.

Intent to feed, the evening flock
spreads and contracts and will not fly
although we flap our scarves
at the fence. A homing cyclist
casts us a puzzled glance.

I don't know why
I think of odd names: kestrel, crane,
catamount, sugarbush, Indian corn.

This was a garden once, and now a scar
from Glastenbury out to high Sierra.
They do not know the names we gave them, moor
and mountain. Far too literate,
we read our image into space.
It is a lone, unsponsored, hungry face.

## The Baptist Owls

Newcomers to my back door
stop and stare
at the southern owl, the only one visible
from this angle. There are four:
Matthew, Mark, Luke, and John I call them,
no longer lion, ox, eagle, man, just steeple-scares
for pigeons, perched still there
at the compass points. By night I hear
the true owl's prey
scream me awake. I think, what bird is that?

Then who's to say
my iron-feathered raptors do not fly
by night, invisibly? Sometimes I wake
with atavistic talons at my throat.
On Jordan's bank (but it is Paran Creek)
my suddenly four-sainted bed sends up
the Baptist's cry. I think,
what bird is that? What bloody bird is that?

## Whitman's

Treasure is where you find it: hay, rope, seed,
halters, dog biscuit, bird-feeders on bleachers
out front, pansies in season, and "Holland Bulbs Are Here,"
the banner says all year. "Mixing and Grinding,"
they call it. But the secret
is the back room. Art can fetch anything

you ever wanted: rat-poison,
compost-enhancer, or horse medicine.

It's a family business.
Bernie's retired. He owns the trillium
woods, up on Matteson. They're thick as snow
come May. Imagination
could not invent them, only memory
out of its back room. How fleeting
a spot of time. But the mind, lingering,
before and after, as it did at Tintern,
sets up a present poetry,
mixing and grinding.


## THE ANCIENT LADIES

On Glastenbury patched with snows
I tell the glacial scars.
The wood is blizzard-bent,
The Roaring Branch is clogged.

I praise the ancient ladies
gone cancerous and crabbed:
my godmother, my final aunt,
a scarf to her bald head.

From weather and from cicatrice
they slide away bright eyes,
and climb the sterile corridors
in their sweet-scented clothes.


## IN MEMORY OF
## FRANCIS FERGUSSON, 1904–1986

> Il temporal foco e l'eterno
> veduto hai, figlio, e sei venuto in parte
> dov' io per me più oltre non discerno.
> —*Purgatorio*, XXVII, 127

When a mind goes, how much we never knew
goes with it. Always singular,
the self in its familiar guises moves
among us, breaking bread,

spending a Sunday on the Battenkill,
hanging its jacket in the hall
crooked. We see, we hear
(but not grandmother in New Mexico;
the daughter has her eyes, the son her furniture)
upon a stage
as spare as Tchekov's. We do not appear
until the second act. We may sit out
three, five (the wintry hair), our own selves getting on,
pasting the picnic at the farm
into the family album. Oh but where
are Aristotle and Shakespeare?

I read of C. S. Peirce, how when he died
they burned his books in the back yard, old Swedenborg
being no use to debtors. No great matter—
far fiercer fires are made of ink and paper.

And this brought back
those afternoons in the Barn. I was nineteen
and wore my skirt on Thursdays. Peirce was there,
Kant, Pascal, Pico, H. James, Jr.,
Cymbeline, Phaedra, Donne—Lord, what a crew
abandoned now like crutches.
      But not so
like kindling, rather, and the afterglow
lighting the secret ways
we selve our works and days.

Some come to Lethe quick.
Some quench the magic
brand before its day. Some flee
across a painted desert. Some sit still
in Barn, in Hall, in Institute,
burning invisibly the will
for bishoprics and honey, burning books. I pray,
*al mio dottor,* they burn
in me. They burn in me.


## BECOMING NOBODY

So that when I die
I shall be nobody, I practice

loss of face. I keep a morning glass
for decency. I wear ghost dress. I bake,
but not for public. Nobody for good,
I'll not want food.

Another way of being nobody
is to be gaudy: popinjay.
Only today
I saw a goldfinch teach its raucous young
to eat my sunflower. Next week
they will not know their mother. Soon
her airy bones will decompose
like angels, when we realize
nor cry nor plume
restores to us, of body born,
that body. I stay on,
keeping my father's house,
like him, gone seasonless.


## To a Friend Dying

Dear one, never approached
but via poetry, or esoteric jokes,
and by reported walks, unshared
except by streams and swallows,
by our inventive Bach, three-part,
played only in private . . .

You've been honored, sir,
above the rest: your Harvard and your war,
your offices, your family affairs, your drink,
your skepticism, your cropped hairs. I think
now of your walking lonely, a false Jew,
well-versed in cautionary tales, select of few.

I am no shepherd of the hills, but in
our mutual green valleys, where the creeks flow
still, and the swallow
sketches her swift inventions, there
they walk with me, the friends I knew,
and with the warbler and the crow,
brother, I walk with you.

## Gone Missing

My mother said, "I miss her
every day of my life."
Think of the princess carried off
to some outlandish keep, the pioneer
forever lost to fair Virginia.
Lot carries on; the looker-back is salt.

Hunters and harpers—they remember pain,
and anecdotes of the hard win
(relics, cattle, women); how they
laid to their breasts and swum. Who stood, who fell
(though some of barley-rigs sing gentle).

Weavers and spinners, those who bear
absence, who croon
the hush-a-bye by night, who knit
prayers, who plant
rosemary, and remember, welcome home
the stravager; those who sacrifice
in secret, those who praise
in secret, wear the locket, keep
the photographs and fires
(though some strike Babylon on golden lyres) . . .

So runs the common legend. Long ago
hag questioned hero: What do women most
desire? He gave a common answer:
power, and won
a common wife, curler,
kohl, and all. It was a tale
told by a chevalier.

She remembers
the day she entered the world, its apple-taste,
its wings, its weathers, and its furtive eyes;
the day she married it, her promise
to keep at home there, and to be at peace
there. What she most desires
is to keep faith (her mother's) under curse
of missing, missing all the way
westward from Moab, over Shenandoah.

## Le Goût d'Ailleurs

Why has elsewhere, why have others
haunted us so? Of blood and breath
little enough, of mockingbird and grass,
the view downstream, the ten-year-old
terrier, the furniture of home.
And still we dream
Rannoch, Wyoming, Rome.
O voyageur!

Is this the charge from Eden,
not to stay? Whatever bade,
I balance in my sixtieth year
(remembering who the angels were)
the coming and the going there, the path
by Rothay and the path by Alph,
the lubber and the sailor self.

I keep a picture of the Yellowstone
tacked to the wall, and that must do
for regions where the muscles shy
and breath comes small, and death
comes fresh. I'll tie
the roses up, like Eve, make where we are
be east and garden, or be west and shore.


## Lots for Sale

There'd be advantages to living in the woods:
no raking leaves.
There'd be the lovely spangled light, the secret
bloodroot, all the woodpeckers,
and where I come from, turkeys. But no view
of Berkshire or Blue Ridge, and no moon rise
on Glastenbury.

Also trees can be
dangerous—Eden lapse,
Algonquin cover. We like a clearing, green
and gardened, with a sycamore or two,
a sunny window.

And still I weep to see them spoiled,
those scions of a former world
we did not make. With fern, with snake,
and all the birds of paradise—
that evidence in Adam's eyes,
those friends of our first tongue—
we kill our brief communion.

Until I do not walk in skin
I need ridge-line to measure by
and woodlot's wild earth-energy,
or else I walk alone.


## Yellowstone Burning

Yellowstone burning, lodgepole pine,
aspen and aster, claw and columbine . . .
Departments check their forest policies
as smoke appals the prairies.

Shoshone simmers, but the weed
will overgreen its ashen scars
where offspring of forgotten wars
may safely graze, and there
the fire-projected seed will root,
and bearberry spring underfoot
and pinescent fill the air.

At Advent in the colonies
imperial conflagrations spread
along the wires, accompanied
already by commercial choirs
crooning of angels and of stars
down every supermarket aisle
where we select our daily bread.
Wise men in orbit overhead
may safely smile.

                I mourn
back-country, as I mourn
burning Jerusalem. But who
hath begotten the drops of dew,
the maple flame, the raven food?
That ranger of the risen wood,

at century's turning, may he keep
a pasture for the mountain sheep,
and for our young the patient light
of burnt-out planets burning.

## Love at Last Sight

A stranger at the door
can make a crone a whore.
What's in a face?
Danger, a breach of peace.

I am done with promises,
ghost voices and ghost flesh,
the crazy nerve that fires
the crazy heart's desires.

The monster in the maze
bellows—it is the last
summons, and the last lust.
I could pick up the thread,
laid female, and betrayed.

But I direct you, whoever you are,
to the neighbor through the hedge,
the possibility, the quest
too little and too late
to correspond with fate.

## To W.B.Y.

I laughed, old Yeats, at your old-age desire
to bring back all your vigor. We all wish
that we could keep the savor with the dish.
I've given away bed-roll and boot.
Not Camelback, Katahdin, or Pine Butte
will I climb again. I think of those Victorian gentlemen
at 80 ready to attack
any odd Swiss or Scottish peak, even Nepal. Ah well,
they kept in good condition,
as you kept poetry, despite some crazy
notion to have it both ways,

the Celtic legend and the London news.
So I've given up
hiking, and the rare companion
even of dog-walks, much less bed and board.
I should be blessed if I could keep the word,

though it make nothing happen—but it made us
happen, and by passionate conception. I could name a few
that I've been daughter to, though they were dead
before I stirred—those toga'd, those be-wigged,
or dog-collared, or blind,
those hymn-singers, those lovers I call friend.
In the public way,
I talk and jostle; in the common plot
take this one's hand, and that one's coat,
but my halt foot
is up Helvellyn, following the great
hill-walkers. Mile by mile
I wilt, I falter. But they never fail.

## Gray's Anatomy

The lilacs' shadows on the Sandys' shed
are intricate as nerves these winter mornings.
Grandfather had *Gray's,* which I inherited
and studied for the sex. Not much
was useful—glands and ducts
and circulation. But I keep old books
around: *The Birds of Britain, Book of Dogs,*
and *The Blue Book of Poetry for Schools.*
These have survived my higher education.

Should I tell
how sex came natural, how genes
bore me, how we have never
got beyond bones, or beat backache
or accident? Not for the present.
Soon stranger shadows may enhance
our light, our lilacs, and our dear nerves' dance.

There are patterns here: the source
of slippery Shenandoah, the long Snake,
the limbs of maples on the winter sky.
There is no asking why.

Ask Cuvier, or Leeuwenhoek,
or lost Lavoisier. They did not know,
nor Gray,
who mapped us like Magellan. But we shift
our shape, our particles, becoming other:
ape, angel, fire-breather.
It is a river
lapping on lands we call our own
some years, and later
years we mark our skeleton
on Sandy's barn.

    The heart
in Gray is ugly, bloody twist
of muscle with its vulgar shoots
like common roots. How do interiors relate
to summer blossoms, or the slow decay
of leafage with some rot
whose name I forget? I think it is not sin. Darwin
might know, who wove the daisy-chain
of being, accurate
as far as it goes. Like Gray,
he drew a bit, but did not mention art.

                      My blunt
shadow is of no interest, nor if all be said,
these clamorous guts I feed
on earth and air and water. But they're other
and kinder shadows. This my word is one.
A second is the canvas hung
on the palazzo walls, all saints
and sunflowers and faces. And a third
that music, never in anatomy,
that heartsease, abstract of our pulsing days.
Master of Shadows, do we shadow you?
He does not tell us, Gray.


## A Winter Gallery

This year: animal tracks
(the rabbit, fox, and deer);
Durham Cathedral taken from below
through icy brush; Vivaldi;

*La Route de la Ferme St.-Siméon, Honfleur*
(Monet); a photo
of Gunpowder Falls in winter; Grand Teton
flushing at dawn; a possum
in a bare tree; the ocean,
Acadia; an *ange* from Amiens;
an oriental duck. These are my post-card offerings
to the kitchen. I have long forgot
who sent them, what they say,
but not how faithfully
my distant friends remember me.

I them, wherever they are: Boonville,
Fincastle, Skokie, Chapel Hill,
and Bennington: survivors all.
We used to sing at school
*Venite,* come, *ad Bethlehem.*

Nor camel king nor pastor, I
take messages at home.
Providing fellowship abide,
a rod and staff are at my side,
whatever journey I must go,
what crux of craft or character,
whatever kingdom come.